BIG DATA

Big Data is everywhere. It shapes our lives in more ways than we know and understand. This comprehensive introduction unravels the complex terabytes that will continue to shape our lives in ways imagined and unimagined.

Drawing on case studies like Amazon, Facebook, the FIFA World Cup and the Aadhaar scheme, this book looks at how Big Data is changing the way we behave, consume and respond to situations in the digital age. It looks at how Big Data has the potential to transform disaster management and healthcare, as well as prove to be authoritarian and exploitative in the wrong hands.

The latest offering from the authors of *Artificial Intelligence: Evolution, Ethics and Public Policy*, this accessibly written volume is essential for the researcher in science and technology studies, media and culture studies, public policy and digital humanities, as well as being a beacon for the general reader to make sense of the digital age.

Saswat Sarangi is a theoretical physicist by training with a PhD from Cornell University, Ithaca, NY, USA. After his PhD, he was a research scientist at Columbia University, New York City, USA. Saswat started his finance career in New York City working as a quant at Bloomberg and later at Citigroup. He currently works with Invesco in Atlanta, USA.

Pankaj Sharma is an engineer from IIT Kharagpur, India, with an MBA from the Faculty of Management Studies, University of Delhi, India. He has more than 15 years of diverse work experience in various leadership roles with global investment banks, Indian equity brokerages, state-owned enterprises and start-ups. Pankaj turned full-time researcher in late 2016 to do in-depth work on contemporary issues. Earlier, he was a ranked equity analyst with UBS, Citi and JP Morgan. Pankaj has also been a regular contributor to print and electronic media.

Pankaj published his first two books in 2017: *Demonetization: Modi's Political Masterstroke* and *2019: Will Modi Win?* This was followed by *Rafale, Raga, Reuniting Forces for 2019* in the second half of 2018 and *The Anatomy of an Indian General Election* in early 2019.

BIG DATA

A Beginner's Introduction

Saswat Sarangi and Pankaj Sharma

Routledge
Taylor & Francis Group

LONDON AND NEW YORK

First published 2020
by Routledge
2 Park Square, Milton Park, Abingdon, Oxon OX14 4RN

and by Routledge
52 Vanderbilt Avenue, New York, NY 10017

Routledge is an imprint of the Taylor & Francis Group, an informa business

British Library Cataloguing-in-Publication Data
A catalogue record for this book is available from the British Library

Library of Congress Cataloging-in-Publication Data
A catalog record has been requested for this book

ISBN: 978-1-138-59857-7 (hbk)
ISBN: 978-0-367-14890-4 (pbk)
ISBN: 978-0-429-33079-7 (ebk)

Typeset in Bembo
by Swales & Willis Ltd, Exeter, Devon, UK

For Richard P. Feynman, there may not be anyone like him again!

CONTENTS

FIGURES

THE STORY BEHIND THIS BOOK

Another mistaken notion connected with the law of large numbers is the idea that an event is more or less likely to occur because it has or has not happened recently. The idea that the odds of an event with a fixed probability increase or decrease depending on recent occurrences of the event is called the gambler's fallacy. That does not happen. For what it's worth, a good streak doesn't jinx you, and a bad one, unfortunately, does not mean better luck is in store.

– *Leonard Mlodinow,* The Drunkard's Walk:
How Randomness Rules Our Lives[1]

I was always late to join the social media bandwagon and it was only about a couple of years ago that I was finally on Facebook and then too sporadically. Somehow the idea of sharing even the most mundane of things happening in your life was not that appealing to me. However, it is always a personal choice and diversity is what makes this world so interesting. Nevertheless, I was so fascinated with the impact of so much data sharing on the individuals and also on society collectively that it became more and more interesting to read and know about.

Space travel to Mars, an inevitable victory of renewable over conventional energy, superhuman artificial intelligence, driverless cars and so many other things which were almost unimaginable even ten years ago are now either reality or close enough. There is just so much happening in the technological space that it is impossible to keep pace. But we don't think keeping pace even matters. We are witnessing so much change and at such a fast pace that this ride in itself is exhilarating. Looking at it closely and soaking up the experience is the next best thing to actually being at the forefront of the development of technology frontiers.

Over the course of researching and writing our previous book, *Artificial Intelligence – Evolution, Ethics and Public Policy*, we became more and more convinced that Big

Data, which is one of the important foundation pillars for the development of AI (artificial intelligence), is an important enough subject in itself, with a lot to discover and understand about this technology and its phenomenal applications. When Aakash Chakrabarty of Taylor & Francis offered us the chance to write about it, we knew we were already passionate about Big Data and wanted to write a book for beginners about it.

The last 50 years – especially after the advent of the personal computer, the ubiquitous Internet and now with smartphones and information technology (IT) in conjunction with rapid developments in communication technology – have fundamentally changed how we live, how we buy, how we eat, how we play, how we make friends and how we source our news and entertainment. The information and communication technology advances have also altered the ways and means of how we interact with each other. We may have become better or worse – that will be subject to a discussion and numerous individual opinions – but there is absolute certainty that we have become different.

This also means that people are generating more data in each subsequent time-frame and these numbers are mind-boggling. But, numbers or data in isolation don't mean much and, wherever there is data, analytics follow to make sense of it. However, when the quantum of data is extremely large and when the data is also unstructured and raw, the conventional tools of data storage and data analysis won't work and will not be very useful. This makes Big Data and Big Data Analytics different from other statistical analyses.[2]

Big Data can be leveraged to make many things better in several areas; and how efficiently and effectively we make use of this unstructured information to first make it structured and then to develop insights, is of paramount importance for the future of humanity. With even bigger challenges, such as seemingly irreversible demographic changes in the world, the worsening climate change situation, the shift in dominant sources of energy and more usage of information technology and significantly better mediums of communication, Big Data can help us in finding solutions to some of the biggest challenges humanity faces. But the story is not that simple.

Big Data can reduce the costs of healthcare, it can make products and services cheaper and better and it can also help law enforcement agencies to catch criminals and reduce terror attacks. In a purely commercial sense, the data gathered has the ability to deliver value for business owners and customers through deep and qualitatively better understanding of customer behavior. Ultimately, it is *How it is and will be used* which determines the end results and effects; that is what matters most for any new advancement in science and technology. And the case is not going to be different with Big Data and Big Data Analytics either.

However, at the same time, Big Data can be a huge risk for an individual's privacy and a massive threat to data security in the hands of hackers and unauthorized agencies. The use of Big Data with a malicious intent can also be used to harm the maturity of public discourse and to manipulate political views. The hidden agenda may not always be detectable and there is a high probability that Big Data can be a dangerous tool in the hands of a demagogue. Since the leaders in Big Data have become so dominant in their industries, another important side effect of Big Data could be the massive gaps in society and huge income inequalities which may be created in the process.

Whether Big Data will be good or bad depends on how the companies and policymakers respond, but Big Data analytics is definitely one of the emerging technologies that is here to stay. This is due to the massive impact it has brought and the even bigger potential it has in its ability to impact differently on our economy, society and humankind in general.

The time to learn more about this amazing technology is here and now. And there is hardly any excuse to postpone this effort for a later date. Big Data as a subject is so interesting that we don't just hope but are also confident that you will enjoy the ride!

Notes

1 Leonard Mlodinow is a popular American science author, screenwriter, physicist and a professor. He has written books on popular science, the screenplay for the 2009 film *Beyond the Horizon* and also for television series including *Star Trek: The Next Generation* and *MacGyver*. *The Drunkard's Walk: How Randomness Rules Our Lives* deals with randomness and people's inability to take it into account in their daily lives. http://leonardmlodinow.com (accessed on 27th April 2019); www.amazon.com/Leonard-Mlodinow/e/B001IGP3W0 (accessed on 27th April 2019).
2 "Big Data Analytics Technology for Beginners" by David Geer. www.ibm.com/developerworks/community/blogs/3ea5ed4d-2e54-439d-bc9f-0ff35757ea5d/entry/Big_Data_Analytics_Technology_for_beginners?lang=en (accessed on 4th December 2017).

ACKNOWLEDGMENTS

For a successful technology, reality must take precedence over public relations, for Nature cannot be fooled.

– *Richard Feynman*[1]

This statement of Richard Feynman during the investigation following the NASA Space Shuttle *Challenger* disaster[2] is one of the most powerful statements we have ever come across.[3] It is something which made an indelible impression on us since we read it for the first time (individually and separately), which was more than 25 years ago. We dedicate this book to Richard Feynman. Not because he was a great scientist, but more because of his utter disregard for bureaucratic procedures and authority and his contribution to making the everyday joy of learning science much more popular and much more fashionable. Feynman lived his entire life by his convictions and by his principles and what a life it was!

Of course, we are not comparing ourselves with him, because Richard Phillips Feynman was quite simply a *rockstar*. He was a great scientist, a teacher par excellence, a visionary and a path-breaking showman, a popular author, a very emotional and passionate human being and much more . . . and all of that rolled into one. But our objective with this book is the same as we try to make some of the more exotic terms, such as Big Data,[4] simpler and less frightening. Technology can be either a friend or an enemy, depending on how we use it.

Our idea is to make the reader in particular, and people in general, more curious about the latest developments in some of these technologies that didn't even exist a couple of decades ago. Many of them are capable of changing the world and whether that will be for good or for bad depends entirely upon how much we understand them. The more we understand and the less we fear, the more chance that we, individually and collectively, will benefit from them. Just like Feynman, we also believe very strongly that curiosity will win us more friends than enemies in technology.

We are immensely grateful to all the teachers, colleagues, professional associates, friends and family members who have not only influenced our thought processes, knowingly or unknowingly, but also helped in molding who we are, as people and as professionals. There are so many of them that it would be virtually impossible to remember each and every one but they all made a significant contribution. We have a deep sense of gratitude towards each and every one of them. Our background research during the writing of our earlier book, *Artificial Intelligence: Evolution, Ethics and Public Policy*, also made us aware of several of these interesting developments and stories concerning Big Data.

Sash would like to thank his wife, Sarmistha and his son, Ishaan. Without their patience this project would not have been possible. Sash would also like to thank his father, Damodar Sarangi and his mother, Annapurna Sarangi, who always encourage him in his pursuit of knowledge. Sash benefited immensely from intellectually stimulating conversations with various experts and non-experts in Cambridge, Massachusetts. He would particularly like to thank Paul O'Connell for bringing to his attention work by Nick Bostrom.[5] Sash would also like to thank various contacts in the financial industry, various friends and acquaintances working in the sales and trading desks of Wall Street banks with whom he had numerous discussions about the impact of automation. A number of these contacts had to, unfortunately, give way to automation and AI, as their jobs required less of the human touch and more of the AI finesse. Roy Rodenstein, with his deep knowledge of technology and his concerns about the human impact of AI, was especially helpful in sharing articles and ideas relevant to a number of topics discussed in this book.

The consent to go ahead and the cooperation of immediate family are never sufficient conditions for an endeavor like this, but they are almost an absolute necessity. Pankaj is deeply thankful to his wife, Shikha and son, Pulin, for their patience and accommodation, keeping in view the enormous demand on Pankaj's time this book warranted during the background research and writing phase. It would not have been possible without the support from them. Pankaj is keen to acknowledge the contribution and encouragement received from many people, so much so that the list below is very long but still incomplete. The first inspiration which comes to his mind was from his maternal grandfather, the late Shri Janardan Shastri "Avaneendra," to whom he would attribute his love for reading and writing. His friends (Sandip Bansal, Saurav Sanyal, Sunil Teluja, Niraj Khare, Rohan Padhi, Rupal Mehrotra, Rohan Arora, Pavitra Kumar, Ramesh Mantri, Sanjeev Soni and Unmesh Sharma), his teachers at Morar, Kharagpur and Delhi (the late Shri Kulwant Singh Sachdeva, Mahavir Sir, Sharma Madam, Bhupendra Sir, Rakesh Sir, Maheshwari Sir, Dr. Gokarn, Dr. Raheja, Dr. Sha, Dr. Ghosh, Dr.Satsangi, Dr.Narag, Dr. Mitra, Dr. Singla, Dr. Pandit and Dr. Kaur, to name a few of them), his workplace superiors at different points in time (Suhas Hari, Suresh Mahadevan, Venkatesh Balasubramaniam, Srikant Bharti, Ashish Gupta, Ajay Garg, Gordon Gray and Kishore Gandhi) and his brothers who provided solid support in this journey (Ranjan Sharma, Neeraj Sharma and Pushkar Shukla). As supportive as these were his parents (Mr. Kamlesh Kumar Sharma/Mrs. Veena Sharma and Dr. Ram Gopal Shukla/Mrs. Mithlesh Shukla). Pankaj would also like to acknowledge the influence of *The Rise of the Robots: Technology and the Threat of Mass Unemployment* by Martin Ford,[6] which played a big role in making him interested in the latest technological developments in Big Data, robotics and artificial intelligence. Pankaj is also grateful to Sumeet Singh and Raghav Kapoor of Smartkarma Innovations,[7] Singapore, for their revolutionary ideas and breakthrough innovations in investment research and providing an efficient and flexible platform for several research analysts, including Pankaj. Pankaj is greatly indebted to Pradip Seth of S-Ancial and ExchangeConnect[8] for openly sharing his ideas and deep expertise on how the new technology and use of Big Data and artificial intelligence could change the flow of information in capital markets and how this evolution will influence the transformation of capital markets ecosystem all over the world.

We wish to acknowledge our sincere gratitude for Mr. Aakash Chakrabarty and Ms. Brinda Sen of Taylor & Francis, whose continuous support and encouragement made this book possible. We were never very good in making a realistic and fair assessment of what the key areas of development were for this book since we submitted the first version of our manuscript, but it was Aakash, Brinda and their team who helped us at each and every step. We are also grateful to all the other team members at Taylor & Francis for their unwavering patience while this book took shape.

We also want to thank Katie Hemmings from Taylor & Frances for nudging us to remain disciplined in meeting all production-process timelines. This section would remain incomplete without acknowledging the contribution of our copy-editor Simon Barraclough. Only when we went through his suggestions and comments on how to improve this text did we realize the pain he has taken to make this book what it is now. Thank you very much, Simon. It has been an enriching experience to work with this entire team and we appreciate your Big contribution to our Big Data work.

Notes

1 Richard Phillips Feynman (1918–1988) was an American theoretical physicist. He studied at the Massachusetts Institute of Technology where he obtained his B.Sc. in 1939, and at Princeton University where he obtained his Ph.D. in 1942. He was Research Assistant at Princeton (1940–1941) and Professor of Theoretical Physics at Cornell University (1945–1950) and the California Institute of Technology (1950–1959). During his lifetime and even after his death, Feynman became one of the best-known scientists in the world. Feynman helped in making physics more popular through his books and lectures: *The Feynman Lectures on Physics*. Feynman also became known

through his semi-autobiographical books, *Surely You're Joking, Mr. Feynman!* and *What Do You Care What Other People Think?* www.nobelprize.org/prizes/physics/1965/feynman/biographical (accessed on 27th April 2019); www.britannica.com/biography/Richard-Feynman (accessed on 27th April 2019).

2 On 28th January 1986, the NASA Space Shuttle *Challenger* broke apart 73 seconds into its flight, killing all seven crew members. The spacecraft disintegrated over the Atlantic Ocean, off the coast of Cape Canaveral, Florida. The disaster resulted in a 32-month hiatus in the Shuttle program and the formation of the Rogers Commission, a special commission appointed by United States President Ronald Reagan to investigate the accident. The Rogers Commission found that NASA's organizational culture and decision-making processes had been key contributing factors to the accident, with the agency violating its own safety rules. www.britannica.com/event/Challenger-disaster (accessed on 27th April 2019); www.space.com/31732-space-shuttle-challenger-disaster-explained-infographic.html (accessed on 27th April 2019).

3 Richard Phillips Feynman was a member of the Rogers Commission, the panel that investigated the NASA Space Shuttle Challenger disaster. Feynman, who was then seriously ill with cancer, was reluctant to undertake the job. At the start of the investigation, fellow members Dr. Sally Ride and General Kutyna gave Feynman a hint that the O-rings were not tested at temperatures below 10°C. During a televised hearing, Feynman demonstrated how the O-rings became less resilient and subject to seal failures at ice-cold temperatures, by immersing a sample of the material in a glass of ice water. He argued that the estimates of reliability offered by NASA management were wildly unrealistic, differing from the estimates of working engineers. "For a successful technology," he concluded, "reality must take precedence over public relations, for nature cannot be fooled." www.feynman.com/science/the-challenger-disaster (accessed on 27th April 2019); www.washingtonpost.com/news/speaking-of-science/wp/2016/01/27/a-famous-physicists-simple-experiment-showed-the-inevitability-of-the-challenger-disaster (accessed on 27th April 2019); https://science.ksc.nasa.gov/shuttle/missions/51-l/docs/rogers-commission/Appendix-F.txt (accessed on 26th February 2018).

4 Big Data is a term for data sets that are so large or complex that traditional data-processing application software is inadequate to deal with them. Big Data challenges include capturing data, data storage, data analysis, searching, sharing, transfering, visualization, querying, updating and keeping information private. Lately, the term "Big Data" tends to refer to the use of predictive analytics, user-behaviour analytics and other advanced data analytics methods that extract value from data. www.sas.com/en_in/insights/big-data/what-is-big-data.html (accessed on 27th April 2019); https://searchdatamanagement.techtarget.com/definition/big-data (accessed on 27th April 2019).

5 Nick Bostrom is a Swedish philosopher known for suggesting that future advances in artificial intelligence research may pose a supreme danger to humanity, if the problem of control has not been solved before super-intelligence is brought into being. He says that although there are potentially great benefits from AI, the problem of control should be the absolute priority. https://nickbostrom.com (accessed on 27th April 2019); www.fhi.ox.ac.uk/team/nick-bostrom (accessed on 27th April 2019).

6 *The Rise of the Robots: Technology and the Threat of Mass Unemployment* by Martin Ford (London: Pan Macmillan, p. 334). As the title suggests, this book is about how artificial intelligence (AI) and more powerful robots are making many blue-collar and white-collar jobs obsolete. The impact of AI not only affects the jobs that are monotonous or can be defined and programmed precisely, but also those that require thinking and judgment. The book also talks about how automation is leading to a scenario where "capital" is becoming the dominant "factor of production." Ford's earlier books include *The Lights in the Tunnel: Automation, Accelerating Technology and the Economy of the Future*. www.amazon.in/Rise-Robots-Technology-Threat-Jobless/dp/1480574775 (accessed on 27th April 2019), https://ig.ft.com/sites/business-book-award/books/2015/winner/the-rise-of-the-robots-by-martin-ford (accessed on 27th April 2019).

7 Smartkarma is a Fintech company servicing the global asset-management industry. It owns and operates a digital marketplace that provides investment insights into Asian markets. Smartkarma is currently the world's only investment-research provider to offer a streaming service. Launched in 2014, Smartkarma is Asia's largest independent marketplace for investment research. www.smartkarma.com/home (accessed on 27th April 2019).

8 ExchangeConnect is an interactive platform to bring one's capital market workflow online. It is a channel for communication between the companies, buy-side fund managers and research teams, sell-side analysts and other sets of investors. S-Ancial integrates artificial intelligence using different technologies (cognitive and semantic) across the industries, from Big Data, business intelligence, analytics, IT technology and others. www.s-ancial.com/about-us (accessed on 27th April 2019); www.exchangeconnect.in/about-exchangeconnect (accessed on 27th April 2019).

INTRODUCTION

> With too little data, you won't be able to make any conclusions that you trust. With loads of data you will find relationships that aren't real . . . Big Data isn't about bits, it's about talent.
>
> – *Douglas Merrill*[1]

One small step for man, one giant leap for mankind

The United States' Apollo 11 was the first manned mission to land on the Moon, on 20th July 1969. However, it is interesting that all of us individually use far more data and computing power today than NASA[2] had available at its disposal in its "Moon Mission." By today's standards, the information technology (IT) NASA used in the Apollo manned lunar program was rudimentary. The setup was no more powerful than a pocket calculator and still did a commendable job in the astronauts' journey from the Earth to the Moon and their safe return in July 1969. The operating method was also very basic, e.g. the Apollo Guidance Computer (AGC) used a real-time operating system, which enabled astronauts to enter simple commands by typing in pairs of nouns and verbs to control the spacecraft.[3]

NASA's technology in the Moon Mission was more basic than the electronics in modern toasters that have computer controlled stop/start/defrost buttons. It only had approximately 64 KB of memory and operated at 0.043MHz. The main-frames were heavily used in the Apollo program with over 3,500 IBM employees also involved. The Goddard Space Flight Center used IBM System/360 Model 75s for communications across NASA and the spacecraft. At the time, IBM described the 6 MB programs it developed, to monitor the spacecrafts' environmental and astronauts' biomedical data, as the most complex software ever written.

But, it is almost unbelievable how things have changed in the last fifty years. Even the simplest of software today would far exceed the technical constraints the Apollo team worked under. That a simple USB memory stick today is much more powerful than the computers that put man on the Moon is testimony to the relentless pace of technological development envisaged in Moore's Law.[4] However, the basic philosophy has remained unchanged. The Apollo program proved that computers could be entrusted with human lives as man and machine worked in unison to achieve what Neil Armstrong[5] termed as "one small step for man, one giant leap for mankind."[6]

The intervening approximately 50 years between "NASA's successful Apollo Moon Mission in July 1969" and "What you can do with your smart phone, here and now" is the story of unbelievable progress in data storage and computing. Fittingly enough, BIG DATA is one of the latest chapters in this story. BIG DATA is not just BIG in its size, it is equally BIG in its impact and the possibilities it creates. BIG DATA is not only already creating new winners and losers, its shadow can be seen on many sectors and this is only going to get bigger. With Big Data and several other associated technological developments, where we as humankind will finally end up cannot be predetermined, but there is little doubt that this journey will be nothing short of absolutely breathtaking.

Information sourcing has changed fundamentally

In the last few decades, the way people source information and get their news and updates has changed. The speed of information dissemination has increased but the cost of receiving it has seen an exponential decline. Another side of this transformation is that easy and instant availability of information has impacted the attention spans of people. In an age when fame is for 15 seconds and people move on very quickly with so many different stimuli competing for their attention, it is very easy for people to get disengaged. This means that brands and personalities have to evolve continuously to stay relevant to an audience, which is extremely demanding and flooded with the incessant bombardment of choices. And when there is so much data, this "reach-out" exercise can't be done manually.

As a concept, there is nothing new in it. For centuries, the access to information and data has been central for the development and growth of civilization and at the same time the evolution of humankind. However, it has reached altogether different dimensions in the 21st century as the collection, processing and use of insights developed from unprecedented volumes of data is redefining all conventional definitions of the way we live. This transformation is not just changing humans' social habits and impacting economic value creation, it has also brought significant competitive advantage for companies which are at forefront of this initiative and have been able to benefit from it.

The 21st century: rise of Big Data, computing power and the cloud

Numerous scientific developments have come together in the new millennium to give technological development a major boost in the field of data. It has become easier to store an ever-increasing amount of data easily and cheaply. The computational

FIGURE 0.1   The Drivers of Exponential Growth in Big Data

resources have become powerful enough to allow easy access and analysis of this data. Over last 20 years, our ability to store, analyze and manipulate tremendous amounts of data has increased by leaps and bounds. This has played a critical role in advancement in Big Data and this technology has become ubiquitous.

Another interesting area is the steep decline in associated costs. The need to own and pay for expensive infrastructure to benefit from Big Data and Analytics has declined considerably with the advent of cloud computing. And a number of mathematical and statistical tools in machine learning have become widely tested and freely available. Access to Big Data, cloud computing and AI-ML (Artificial Intelligence-Machine Leaning) has also become democratized, with researchers and companies willing to share information. The easy accessibility to Big Data methods, cloud computing and computational methods can potentially make progress even faster.

Big Data – explosion of data in the new millennium

In the previous century, almost all the information was stored in analog containers such as books, disks, magnetic tapes, etc. As the new millennium started, and the world was fixated on solving the Y2K problem, digital storage swiftly replaced analog devices as the preferred medium for information and data storage. The world's capacity to store information has increased drastically over the last 20 years, exploding from approximately 2 billion gigabytes in the mid-1980s, to over 300 billion gigabytes by late 2007.[7] Extrapolating this trend from 2007 to 2017 would give a figure of around a trillion gigabytes in 2017.

The current storage capacity is likely to be even greater, given the massive information explosion that has accompanied social media. This is a mind-numbing number for the amount of data, but what is impressive is how easily accessible it is to anyone with access to even a smartphone. What sets our present time apart from previous ones is the ease with which laypersons, not just the experts, can access Big Data and use it, and, if possible, benefit from it. The cost of storing data has come down tremendously. The cost of the storage of 1 GB of data was about $438K in 1980, $11K in 1990 and just $11 in 2000. In 2014 this cost was just three cents. Now, in 2017, Google offers free storage for up to 15 GB of data.

Computational power

An increase in data-storage capability would not mean much, unless accompanied by an increase in the computational power to manipulate the data. Indeed, there has been about a trillion-fold increase in the processing power of computers from the 1950s to 2017. To understand how much computing power is at a layperson's fingertips, consider the fact that a single Apple iPhone 5 has 2.7 times the processing power of the 1985 Cray-2 supercomputer – a thought which would have been unbelievable in the mid-1980s. Another example showing the speed of development in computation is the Samsung Galaxy S6, which is the equivalent of five PlayStation 2s in terms of processing power. Computing power has not only exponentially increased; it has become easily available to the common people.[8]

Cloud computing

The final development leading to the democratization of data and computation is the evolution of cloud-based computing. With the advent of the cloud, infrastructure can be delivered as a service. There is no need to own the complex infrastructure required to store Big Data and slice and dice it. One can access data, as well as the tools to analyze that data, by accessing the cloud. It has become possible for a reasonably smart school student to open an Amazon or Google cloud service account, and do serious analysis on it. It has also become possible for small start-ups to very quickly begin exploring projects without the need to set up the computing infrastructure or employ personnel to maintain that infrastructure. This has allowed for new developments to occur at an even faster rate.

The impact of Big Data, computing power and cloud computing

Big Data, computing power and cloud computing, have all been important in making huge amounts of data and enormous computing power available for anyone who is interested. All these developments may seem unconnected at first but they were not just happening in parallel but also, in some ways, feeding into each other. For example, unless there is storage available for large data, computing capability may not progress that fast or vice versa, i.e. unless you can use and process these large volumes of data with the help of faster, more efficient computing, the large volumes of data storage may not be helpful.

After discussing the basic building blocks for Big Data Analytics and looking at the fact that there is a lot of network effect in play (the network effect is a phenomenon whereby every additional user of a service or product increases the value in a disproportionately higher quantum), we will look at some of the important characteristics which make Big Data different from our other regular information and data in the next sections of this chapter. We will also discuss how it is impacting more and more industries and where the future might take us on Big Data.

More information = more data, more data = more analytics

More information also requires a more proactive effort to store, analyze and understand the available data. The large amount of data or "Big Data" has now reached almost every sector in society and the economy. In the case of the economy, it competes with other essential factors of production, such as capital and labor, and in the context of society it has become the "change agent" for how we interact with each other in the real world and in the virtual world. Nevertheless, we have just scratched the surface of the possibilities which can open up because of Big Data.

A growing majority of businesses are now seeking to leverage data as a critical strategic asset, helping to uncover new sources of business value – and Big Data is playing a critical role in business strategy.[9] However, the use of Big Data and Analytics transcends sectors and it can help in: (a) creating more transparency by making information more easily available, (b) understanding the ways and means to improve the efficiency and effectiveness of policies and (c) segmenting specific populations to customize actions in order to meet their precise needs.

Why Big Data is Big Data

Big Data is defined by three Vs: volume (amount of data), velocity (speed of data in and out) and variety (range of data types and sources). Big Data is high-volume, high-velocity and/or high-variety information which can be used for decision-making after processing. The data must be processed with advanced analytics to reveal meaningful insights. Since the data is large and mostly in an unstructured form, it is critical to process it quickly and correctly so that actionable insights can be drawn which can improve the results.[10]

For Big Data applications to be useful, the data needs to be stored, processed and delivered in a comprehensible format, so that it can be used effectively. The dramatic increase in data-storage capacity, combined with much faster and efficient computing capabilities, has played a critical role in advancement of Big Data Analytics. The advance algorithm is certainly the backbone but without the supporting hardware, it may not have worked as intended. The parallel developments in several areas have contributed to the evolution and growth of Big Data.

As we have seen in the previous section, "The 21st century: rise of Big Data, computing power and the cloud," the advancements have been rapid with significant changes occurring in almost every decade. For example, from a bulky and difficult to handle 1.2 MB to 1.44 MB floppy disk (8-inch, 5¼-inch and 3½-inch floppy disks) to the early years of the 21st century, to pen drives today which can carry 64 GB, the amount of data that can be carried reliably, cheaply and efficiently has grown exponentially. All these changes have contributed to the 3Vs.

How accurate are the inferences drawn from Big Data?

There are two broad methods of reasoning, which are deductive and inductive approaches. These two methods of reasoning are characteristically different. Inductive reasoning is open-ended and exploratory and leads to possibilities hitherto unexplored. While on the other hand deductive reasoning is narrow and is only concerned with testing and confirming or disproving hypotheses. Big Data

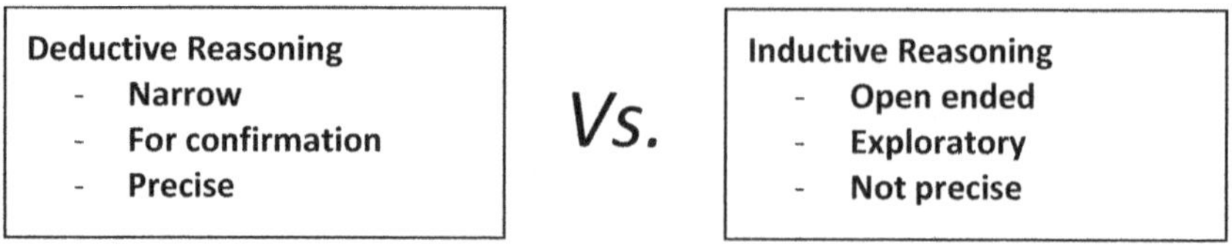

Deductive Reasoning		Inductive Reasoning
- Narrow - For confirmation - Precise	*Vs.*	- Open ended - Exploratory - Not precise

FIGURE 0.2 Deductive Reasoning vs. Inductive Reasoning

Analytics is not a precise science because it is not based on deductive reasoning and works mostly on inductive reasoning. This makes Big Data prone to mistakes in terms of inferences drawn from it, so actionable insights will also tend to vary.

Big Data works through looking at a large set of data followed by pattern recognition and then offering insights and making recommendations. The process is that of inductive reasoning, hence Big Data is not yet at a stage where it can deliver a 100% foolproof solution. Even when you are interested in employing the services of Big Data, it is not always certain that it will work in a desired and expected manner. Secondly, the analytics tools are only as good as the data they are using. Moreover, there are times when not everything can be captured in data and when not everything that data is capturing will be important.

There are some famous examples where the data collected was not truly representative for the analysis of the problem in hand and though there was nothing wrong in the data collection and the algorithms used, the net result was a disaster. For the insights to be really useful, there is a need to apply serious thought before managers and decision-makers can freeze the variables, including what data will be collected, how it will be collected, for how long it will be collected and how it will be processed. "More data" will not always mean "better data" or "more useful data" and the decision-makers need to be wary of these pitfalls.

The path from unstructured data to actionable insights

The typical process for data analytics is as follows: **Unstructured Data –> Data Capture –> Data Sorting –> Structured Data –> Data Analysis –>Actionable Insights –> Predictive Models –> Future Forecast –> Results Evaluation –> Process Modifications**. One of the important issues with Big Data is that the data is so vast that looking for meaningful and actionable reference points is like looking for a needle in a haystack. Moreover, the data will be in an unstructured format, which means that it is hard to see any patterns in it unless it becomes sorted and more structured. If we want to understand and interpret Big Data, the datasets must first be made manageable.

This is a cumbersome process and time is of the essence because the analysis has to be done on a real-time basis and the recommendations need to be incorporated and acted upon quickly. After that, even if we have insights, it may not actually be enough for us to change our business strategy in such a way that adds value.

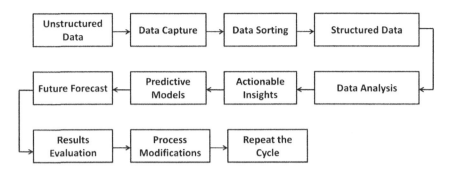

FIGURE 0.3   The Cycle for Data and its Analysis

The data is only there to assist in business decisions but it is the managers who will take these calls and the quality of these calls is as much dependent on the interpretation of this data. The cost vs. benefit analysis and the feasibility of decisions will be important criteria before a definite conclusion can be drawn.

There is another challenge for managers and decision-makers. Every decision has a consequence and each consequence has several side effects. These unintended side effects are called second-order effects. Every decision will have these second-order effects and managers have to be careful because their decisions may have the opposite effect of what they aim for. Big Data Analytics will not be able to throw much light on many of these second-order effects and it is the responsibility of decision-makers to consider all aspects before they move forward with a decision. This clearly implies that neither Big Data nor analytics can be trusted blindly.

Big Data Applications: they are everywhere

Amazon[11] is one of the prime examples of analytics success stories. They were early adopters in analyzing personal information from customers and using predictive analytics for targeted marketing to increase customer satisfaction for enhanced profitability. Another example is Facebook.[12] Facebook is one of the most valuable public companies in the world, with a market value in the hundreds of billion dollars because it has so much data. Facebook is not in the business of connecting the world or facilitating your interactions with your friends, it is in the business of data analytics, so that it can use the information it has on you.

There are several more Big Data success stories, ranging from Germany winning the 2014 FIFA World Cup and Big Data helping Barack Obama[13] in winning the US Presidential Elections. For all of us, it is vital to understand how much a customer matters and there are several possible data points of relevance, including location, age, past behavior, interests, activity time, brand interaction, purchasing power, habits and more.

There are more than commercial reasons to feel excited about the potential utilization of Big Data. For example, personalized information about an individual, including his or her genetic analysis and DNA analysis is already being used to detect the likelihood of contracting a disease and the risks of specific conditions. With the help of this data, people can take preventive steps to avoid behavior which might increase their risk of getting a disease or an undesirable medical condition. There are already molecular-diagnostics companies that are doing this to make people more aware about their health. These companies offer personalized recommendations based on genetic tests and diagnosis. This is a big enhancement in preventive healthcare.[14]

Authorities and governments with the right intentions and who want to be accountable are already (and if not, they will be shortly) using data to measure everything. To start with, policymakers need to ensure that their intentions are good, which in itself is a big challenge, at times, to continuously monitor and address. Once they have a good handle on data capture and analysis, they are able to set goals and compare results and accomplishments against expectations or targets. There are already several governments and administrative bodies using data to devise better policies and a more effective response from the administration. If the processes are streamlined, more data is captured in an efficient manner and this data is then used to devise better policies without bias. Some of the developing countries in Asia and Africa can benefit much more than developed countries.

Big Data = competitive advantage

The ownership of Big Data and the ability to analyze it well is becoming a major competitive advantage for corporations. Across sectors, leaders in the collection and analysis of Big Data are getting bigger and more profitable. The advantage of a lead in Big Data will help in creating new growth opportunities and new winners and losers. Early movers are likely to reap the most benefits as there will be a significant increase in efficiency and productivity. There is also a link between Big Data Analytics and innovation, as the use of Big Data Analytics is associated with a higher propensity to innovate, as well as higher innovation intensity.

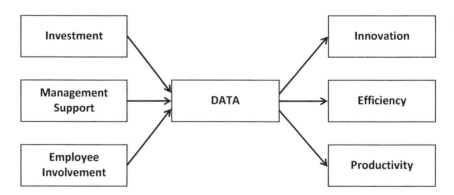

FIGURE 0.4 Data – What it Needs and What it Does for an Organization

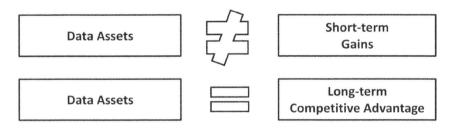

FIGURE 0.5   Data Assets – Source of Competitive Advantage

Research has already proved that investments in activities such as data security and standardization generate more value in the context of a firm that has made early investments in data collection. This observation suggests that managers should recognize and consider the value of these assets, even if they do not produce short-term performance gains. From a strategic perspective, these findings have important managerial implications because databases are often costly to produce and curate. Therefore, the results suggest that considerable data assets that have been developed by many firms pose a significant source of competitive advantage to these firms.

Urban planners and crowd-management authorities can significantly benefit from the analysis of personal location data. The data can be used to cut congestion and can help in managing large-scale human movements. The use of Big Data on a real-time basis can alert the authorities to situations which might arise because of temporary weather factors, or an unexpected bottleneck. The use of Big Data doesn't necessarily mean that disasters may be averted but the loss of lives and injuries would certainly come down.

The challenges

In many cases, the real challenge is how to move forward with Big Data and how to give data analytics a prominent role. Unfortunately, the truth is that there are no ready-made, straightforward answers to some of the questions that any organization struggles with. These questions include: (a) why do they need to gather data and what type of data should be collected? (b) how should it be analyzed and be used to produce actionable insights? and (c) how to measure return on investment (ROI) in these technologies? The corporations need to make choices which have long-term implications and they have to optimize the variables in decision-making.

The major problem many organizations face is that there is a lot of confusion about Big Data and multiple viewpoints on how it should be handled; who will be the best fit among vendors; how to choose the internal teams to lead the projects; how much it will cost and what are the expected tangible benefits? With the lack of understanding on core issues and unrealistic expectations, there be no informed decision by managers and that means that the Big Data experience of

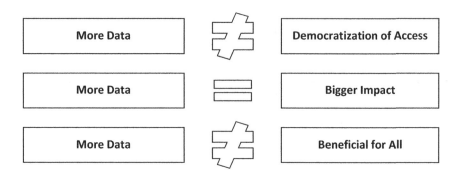

FIGURE 0.6 Is Data Leading to More Inequality?

these organizations will be sub-optimal. To some extent, the blame in this case should also lie with the Big Data vendors who will promise the Moon and only highlight successful pilots and case studies.

Another important challenge for governments and policymakers is that it is important to work towards the democratization of access to Big Data, so that the benefits don't remain confined to a particular section of society or the economy. Because of "the winner takes all"[15] nature of these industries in general, it becomes even more critical that sincere efforts are made to curtail the inequality which is being created between the "haves" and "have nots" when it comes to data and analytics. Unless we see more equitable gains, there is always a high probability that fissures in society will emerge and that will lead to catastrophic consequences sooner or later.

There are also issues with the assertion that Big Data will be equally beneficial across sectors and across verticals in organizations. This is highly unlikely. For example, the kind of impact Big Data can make in the financial services industry or in the retail sector, will take much longer to realize similar kinds of benefits in manufacturing or in agriculture. The relative dependency on different sectors and hence the potential benefits for an organization, for an economy, for a society and for a country are different. How much Big Data will be optimal depends on which stage you are at in the evolution cycle and this will be the key to making best use of Big Data.

The privacy debate

As Big Data become more important, the policy issues linked to privacy and data security have become more crucial. Collecting the data is the easier part but the bigger challenge is the protection of privacy and the security of sensitive information. It is easy to see that as more data is stored, the more vital it is to ensure its security. Hackers' attacks on IT systems are becoming more lethal and new viruses and security breaches are ever-more powerful. This requires a coordinated response and companies have to face these issues on a daily basis.

A lack of data security can lead to great financial losses and reputational damage for a company. How to protect sensitive data is of the utmost importance as incidents related to data leaks have demonstrated. It is no surprise that many citizens and organizations around the world regard this collection of massive amounts of data and information with deep suspicion and skepticism because they think it is a serious intrusion of their privacy. Personal data, being the most sensitive, is always under the threat of being leaked.

The Aadhaar[16] issued by the Unique Identification Authority of India (UIDAI) is a prime example of how an innovative identification scheme, which also has biometric data, can have the security of its data threatened and therefore the privacy of citizens is also threatened. Aadhaar is a 12-digit unique-identity number issued to all Indian residents based on their biometric and demographic data. The data is collected by the UIDAI and Aadhaar is the world's largest biometric ID system, with over 1.171 billion enrolled members as of 15 Aug 2017. There are several issues with AADHAAR but the biggest of them all is data security and privacy.

The amount of detailed personal information being collected is extremely important to an individual. However, once collected, it is not being treated with the required sensitivity of privacy concerns. Major financial transactions are linked to information collected in AADHAR. Data leaks are a great opportunity for hackers and criminals. There is a big question as to whether the government department and various other agencies that collect and use this data, including banks, etc., can be trusted to maintain the secrecy of all this collected information. There have been instances when AADHAR data collected by some private companies was leaked online.

No turning back

Big Data is a technology which is leading to serious disruptions and significant changes in how governments and organizations function. It also plays a key role in the case of individuals, either knowingly or unknowingly, and whether the permission for such data to be used is a conscious decision or not. Big Data has made an impact across industries including retail, healthcare, the delivery of public services and politics. It has also been observed that, in most cases, the use of Big Data is not a choice anymore. You either have to jump on the bandwagon or be left behind. In the case of companies, apart from an increased top line and better profitability, Big Data is also responsible for creating competitive advantages and could also be a source of innovation.

However, as happens with most other technologies, there are also challenges and most of them are linked with the understanding and implementation of what Big Data can do and what it cannot. There are also cases when vendors lure organizations by making far-fetched promises and setting unrealistic expectations. It is hardly a surprise that many of the Big Data success stories are either sponsored by vendors or are examples of sensationalized reporting where gains and contributions to the bottom line are magnified and exaggerated, if not completely baseless.

Hence, we believe that a regular cost–benefit analysis and follow-up on progress is an absolutely integral part of Big Data Analytics.

Having said this, and after we have identified and discussed the important bottle necks in realizing the true potential of Big Data, we need to make a candid admission. Despite the many perils of the modern lifestyle, we can't go back to the lifestyle of the "cave man" and can't return to the pre-electricity era or stop using air travel and the Internet. Similarly, we cannot and will not turn back the clock on Big Data. Big Data is not a fad; it is a transformative technological innovation which has solid foundations and an extremely compelling business case.

It will not only be able to sustain its importance, there is no doubt at all in our minds that Big Data will increase in its influence and importance. If there is anything certain about Big Data, it is the fact that it is here to stay and to grow.

Notes

1 Douglas Clark Merrill is an American technologist and businessman. He is the CEO and founder of ZestFinance (formerly ZestCash), a Los Angeles-based financial services technology company that uses machine learning and data science to help companies make credit decisions. Previously, Merrill was CIO at Google from 2003–2008 and served as president of EMI Music's digital unit from 2008–2009. In March 2010, Merrill published the book, *Getting Organized in the Google Era: How to Get Stuff Out of Your Head, Find It When You Need It, and Get It Done Right* (New York: Broadway Books, 2010) www.crunchbase.com/person/douglas-merrill#section-overview (accessed on 27th April 2019).

2 The National Aeronautics and Space Administration (NASA) is a US agency for the civilian space program, as well as aeronautics and aerospace research. The agency became operational on 1st October 1958. www.nasa.gov (accessed on 27th April 2019).

3 "Apollo 11: The computers that put man on the moon" by Cliff Saran. www.computerweekly.com/feature/Apollo-11-The-computers-that-put-man-on-the-moon (accessed on 4th December 2017).

4 Moore's Law is the observation that the number of transistors in a dense integrated circuit doubles approximately every two years. The observation is named after Gordon Moore, the co-founder of Fairchild Semiconductor and Intel, whose 1965 paper described a doubling every year in the number of components per integrated circuit and projected that this rate of growth would continue for at least another decade. In 1975, looking forward to the next decade, he revised the forecast to doubling every two years. "Moore's Law" reviewed by Carla Tardi, updated 20th April 2019. www.investopedia.com/terms/m/mooreslaw.asp (accessed on 27th April 2019).

5 Neil Armstrong (1930–2012) was an American pilot and astronaut who commanded the Apollo 11 Moon landing mission on 20th July, 1969. Armstrong was the first human to walk on the moon. www.nasa.gov/audience/forstudents/k-4/.../who-was-neil-armstrong-k4.html (accessed on 27th April 2019), https://www.britannica.com/biography/Neil-Armstrong (accessed on 27th April 2019).

6 "July 20, 1969: One giant leap for mankind." www.nasa.gov/mission_pages/apollo/apollo11.html (accessed on 4th December 2017). "That's one small step for 'a' man": Armstrong claimed his famous mankind speech was misquoted. www.dailymail.co.uk/news/article-2193749/Neil-Armstrong-speech-Thats-small-step-man-famous-mankind-words-misquoted.html (accessed on 27th April 2019).

7 "The world's technological capacity to store, communicate and compute information" by M. Hilbert and P. Lopez. www.martinhilbert.net/worldinfocapacity-html (accessed on 26th October 2017).

8 "Processing power compared." https://pages.experts-exchange.com/processing-power-compared (accessed on 26th October 2017).

9 "When Big Data is a big headache: Addressing the challenges to reap rewards" by Darren Watkins. www.itproportal.com/features/when-big-data-is-a-big-headache-addressing-the-challenges-to-reap-rewards (accessed on 2nd December 2017).

10 The 3Vs (volume, variety and velocity) are defining properties or dimensions of Big Data. Volume refers to the amount of data, variety refers to the number of types of data and velocity refers to the speed of data processing. Gartner analyst Doug Laney introduced the 3Vs concept in 2001 in the MetaGroup research publication, "3D Data Management: Controlling Data Volume, Variety and Velocity." http://whatis.techtarget.com/definition/3Vs (accessed on 26th February 2018).

11 Amazon.com is an American electronic-commerce and cloud-computing company based in Seattle, Washington that was founded by Jeff Bezos on 5th July 1994. It is the largest Internet retailer in the world, as measured by revenue and market capitalization and the second largest after the Alibaba Group in terms of total sales. www.amazon.com (accessed on 27th April 2019).

12 Facebook is an American online social media and social networking service company based in Menlo Park, California. The Facebook website was launched on 4th February 2004, by Mark Zuckerberg, along with fellow Harvard College students. Facebook has more than two billion monthly active users as of June 2017. www.facebook.com (accessed on 27th April 2019).

13 In the 2008 US Presidential elections, Barack Obama was elected President. In 2012, after winning re-election by defeating his Republican opponent Mitt Romney, Obama was sworn in for a second term. www.britannica.com/event/United-States-presidential-election-of-2008 (accessed on 27th April 2019), https://www.britannica.com/event/United-States-Presidential-Election-of-2012 (accessed on 27th April 2019).

14 "What consumer DNA data can and can't tell you about your risk for certain diseases. Consumers face lots of choices and unanswered questions" by Tina Hesman Saey. www.sciencenews.org/article/health-dna-genetic-testing-disease (accessed on 27th April 2019).

15 A winner-takes-all market is a market in which the best performers are able to capture a very large share of the rewards and the remaining competitors are left with very little. www.merriam-webster.com/dictionary/winner%20takes%20all (accessed on 26th February 2018).

16 The Unique Identification Authority of India (UIDAI) is a statutory authority established under the provisions of the AADHAAR (Targeted Delivery of Financial and Other Subsidies, Benefits and Services) Act, 2016 (Aadhaar Act 2016). It was enacted on 12th July 2016 by the Government of India under the Ministry of Electronics and Information Technology (MeitY). The first UID number was issued on 29th September 2010 to a resident of Nandurbar, Maharashtra. The total number of enrolments to date is more than 120 crore (A crore equals ten million). https://uidai.gov.in/about-uidai/unique-identification-authority-of-india/about.html (accessed on 27th April 2019).

1

BIG DATA

What, why and how

Information is the oil of the 21st century, and analytics is the combustion engine.
— *Peter Sondergaard*[1]

Amazon: In the business of selling or in the business of data?[2]

Amazon is one of the prime examples of analytics success stories. They were one of the early adopters and are leaders in collecting, storing, processing and analyzing personal information from customers as a means of determining how customers are spending their money. The company uses predictive analytics and proprietary algorithms for targeted marketing to increase customer satisfaction and build company loyalty. Amazon's recommendations are based on customers' in-depth profiles and are a great example of what can be achieved with data analytics. The methods have evolved and are getting more sophisticated but the underlying concept is the same: the traditional objectives of marketing, which are selling more and selling better can be helped by using data analytics. Amazon analyzes which items customers purchased previously, what is in their online shopping cart, what they search for and, on the basis of that, what they may buy in future. This information is used to recommend products, hence Amazon uses the power of suggestion to encourage you to buy more and this increases the company's revenue significantly. There are other methods as well. On the basis of the words highlighted in Kindle by a reader, Amazon may send you more book recommendations.

Amazon also has an anticipatory shipping model which uses Big Data for predicting which products customers are likely to purchase and when. Amazon uses analytics to increase its product sales and profit margins while decreasing its delivery time and expenses. Because Amazon wants to fulfill orders quickly, the company links with manufacturers and tracks their inventory. Amazon uses Big Data systems for choosing the warehouse, best delivery schedule, route and product groupings to reduce shipping costs.

The next one is a little more controversial. Big Data is also used for managing Amazon's prices to increase profits. Prices are set according to your activity on the website, competitors' pricing, product availability, item preferences, order history and other factors. Product prices typically change very quickly as Big Data is updated and analyzed. The pricing is individualized. Amazon also sells these services through Amazon Web Services and companies can use Big Data to benefit by analyzing customer demographics and spending habits.

It is not an exaggeration to say that Amazon is not in the business of selling goods to you, it is in the business of data analytics so that it can sell better . . . not just today . . . but, tomorrow, the day after and forever.

What is Big Data?

The *Oxford Dictionary* defines Big Data as[3] "Extremely large data sets that may be analyzed computationally to reveal patterns, trends, and associations, especially relating to human behavior and interactions."

In its June 2011 report titled *Big Data: The next frontier for innovation, competition, and productivity*, McKinsey Global Institute defined Big Data as:[4]

> "Big Data" refers to datasets whose size is beyond the ability of typical database software tools to capture, store, manage, and analyze. This definition is intentionally subjective and incorporates a moving definition of how big a dataset needs to be in order to be considered Big Data – i.e., we don't define Big Data in terms of being larger than a certain number of terabytes (thousands of gigabytes). We assume that, as technology advances over time, the size of datasets that qualify as Big Data will also increase. Also note that the definition can vary by sector, depending on what kinds of software tools are commonly available and what sizes of datasets are common in a particular industry. With those caveats, Big Data in many sectors today will range from a few dozen terabytes to multiple petabytes (thousands of terabytes).

Essentially, Big Data is a term which is used to mean a massive volume of both structured and unstructured data that is so large that it is difficult to process using traditional database and software techniques. In most enterprise scenarios the volume of data is too big, or it moves too fast, or it exceeds current processing capacity.[5] Interestingly, it is difficult to agree upon a standard definition because different people will use the term Big Data in different contexts and that will determine what they mean when they talk about "Big Data."

When someone is talking about data-storage capacity, Big Data means the size or volume of the data. When the computing capability is under discussion, Big Data perhaps means the processing capability when discussing computing. The vendors specializing in this technology will refer to the technology and tools which will be used to analyze this data when they talk about Big Data. Organizations will talk more about data generation and accumulation when they mention Big Data. However, there are certain characteristics of Big Data which will be there most of the time and they are: size, unstructured nature and the need for processing to make sense of it.

The history

The term Big Data has been in use since the 1990s, with some giving credit to John Mashey for coining it, or at least making it popular. Big Data encompasses unstructured, semi-structured and structured data, however, the main focus is on unstructured data. Big Data "size" is a constantly moving target as storage capacity increases and processing gets faster.[6]

In a 2001 research report[7] and related lectures, META Group (now Gartner) defined data-growth challenges and opportunities as being three-dimensional i.e. increasing **volume** (amount of data), **velocity** (speed of data in and out) and **variety** (range of data types and sources). Most of the industry continue to use this volume, velocity and variety (or 3Vs model) for describing Big Data. In 2012, Gartner updated its definition as follows: "Big Data is high-volume, high-velocity and/or high-variety information assets that demand cost-effective, innovative forms of information processing that enable enhanced insight, decision making, and process automation."[8]

For the last few years, we have also started to see and use the concept of 4Vs (including the fourth one called *Veracity* implying that Big Data could have ambiguities and uncertainties because of the nature of the data) or 5Vs (*Veracity* and *Value*, implying that Big Data will need to be associated with meaningful benefits to have value) of Big Data. However, Gartner's definition of the 3Vs is still widely used and is in agreement with a consensual definition that states that[9] "Big Data represents the Information assets characterized by such a High Volume, Velocity and Variety to require specific Technology and Analytical Methods for its transformation into Value." The 3Vs have been expanded to other complementary characteristics of Big Data:[10]

Volume: Big Data doesn't sample; it just observes and tracks what happens.

Velocity: Big Data is often available in real time.

Variety: Big Data draws from text, images, audio, video; plus it completes missing pieces through data fusion.

Machine learning: Big Data often doesn't ask why and simply detects patterns.

Digital footprint: Big Data is often a cost-free byproduct of digital interaction.

The data must be processed with advanced tools (analytics and algorithms) to reveal meaningful information so that both visible and invisible issues with various components can be considered and taken into analysis.[11]

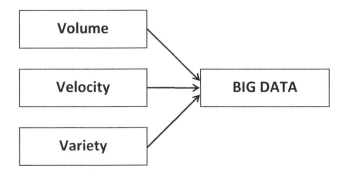

FIGURE 1.1   The Three Vs of Big Data

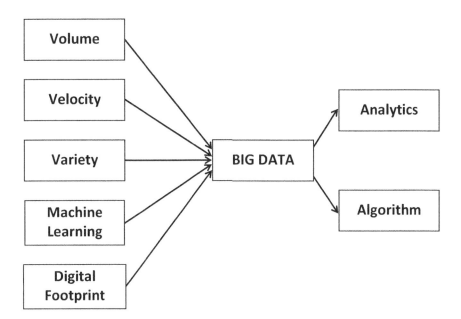

FIGURE 1.2   Big Data – The Characteristics and Processing

The terminology[12]

In the context of Big Data, the first term is data storage. The different units of data measurement describe disk space, or data-storage space and system memory and this is evolving very fast. From a bulky and difficult-to-handle 1.2 MB to 1.44 MB floppy disk (8-inch, 5¼-inch and 3½-inch floppy disks) up until the early years of the 21st century, to pen drives today, which can easily carry 64 GB.

According to the *IBM Dictionary of Computing*, when used to describe disk storage capacity, a megabyte is 1,000,000 bytes in decimal notation. But when the term megabyte is used for real and virtual storage and channel volume, 2 to the 20th power or 1,048,576 bytes is the appropriate notation. According to the *Microsoft Press Computer Dictionary*, a megabyte means either 1,000,000 bytes or 1,048,576 bytes. According to Eric S. Raymond in *The New Hacker's Dictionary*, a megabyte is 1,048,576 bytes on the argument that bytes should be computed in powers of 2.

The 1,000 can be replaced with 1,024 and still be correct using the other acceptable standards. For the processor or virtual storage:

> 1 bit = binary digit, 8 bits = 1 byte, 1,024 bytes = 1 kilobyte, 1,024 kilobytes = 1 megabyte, etc.

For the disk storage:

> 1 bit = binary digit, 8 bits = 1 byte, 1,000 bytes = 1 kilobyte, 1,000 kilobytes = 1 megabyte, etc.

Bit: A Bit is the smallest unit of data that a computer uses. It can be used to represent two states of information, such as Yes or No.

Byte: A Byte is equal to 8 Bits. A Byte can represent 256 states of information, for example, numbers or a combination of numbers and letters. 1 Byte could be equal to one character. 10 Bytes could be equal to a word. 100 Bytes would equal an average sentence.

Kilobyte: A Kilobyte is approximately 1,000 Bytes, actually 1,024 Bytes, depending on which definition is used. 1 Kilobyte would be equal to this paragraph you are reading, whereas 100 Kilobytes would equal an entire page.

Megabyte: A megabyte is approximately 1,000 Kilobytes. In the early days of computing, a megabyte was considered to be a large amount of data. These days

TABLE 1.1 Data storage

Unit	Short Name	Full Name
1 Bit	Bit	Binary Digit
8 Bit	1 Byte	Byte
2^{10} i.e.1,024 Bytes	1 KB	Kilobyte
2^{10} i.e.1,024 KB	1 MB	Megabyte
2^{10} i.e.1,024 MB	1 GB	Gigabyte
2^{10} i.e.1,024 GB	1 TB	Terrabyte
2^{10} i.e.1,024 TB	1 PB	Petabyte
2^{10} i.e.1,024 PB	1 EB	Exabyte
2^{10} i.e.1,024 EB	1 ZB	Zettabyte
2^{10} i.e.1,024 ZB	1 YB	Yottabyte
2^{10} i.e.1,024 YB	1 Brontobyte	Brontobyte
2^{10} i.e.1,024 Brontobytes	1 Geopbyte	Geopbyte

Source: http://whatsabyte.com (Accessed on 7th December 2017)

with a 500-Gigabyte hard drive on a computer being common, a megabyte doesn't seem like much anymore. One of those old 3–1/2 inch floppy disks can hold 1.44 Megabytes or the equivalent of a small book. 100 Megabytes might hold a couple volumes of Encyclopedias. 600 Megabytes is about the amount of data that will fit on a CD-ROM disk.

Gigabyte: A Gigabyte is approximately 1,000 Megabytes. A Gigabyte is still a very common term used these days when referring to disk space or drive storage. 1 Gigabyte of data is almost twice the amount of data that a CD-ROM can hold. But it's about one thousand times the capacity of a 3–1/2 floppy disk. 1 Gigabyte could hold the contents of about ten yards of books on a shelf. 100 gigabytes could hold the entire library floor of academic journals.

Terabyte: A Terabyte is approximately one trillion bytes, or 1,000 gigabytes. This was unimaginable even a few years back but now 1 and 2 terabyte drives are the normal specs for many new computers. A Terabyte could hold about 3.6 million 300 Kilobyte images or about 300 hours of good quality video. A Terabyte could hold 1,000 copies of the Encyclopedia Britannica. 10 Terabytes could hold the printed collection of the Library of Congress.

Petabyte: A Petabyte is approximately 1,000 Terabytes or one million gigabytes. It's hard to visualize what a Petabyte could hold. 1 Petabyte could hold approximately 20 million 4-door filing cabinets full of text. It could hold 500 billion pages of standard printed text. It would take about 500 million floppy disks to store the same amount of data.

Exabyte: An Exabyte is approximately 1,000 Petabytes. Another way to look at it is that an Exabyte is approximately one quintillion bytes or one billion gigabytes. There is not much to compare an Exabyte to. It has been said that 5 Exabytes would be equal to all of the words ever spoken by mankind.

Zettabyte: A Zettabyte is approximately 1,000 Exabytes. There is nothing to compare a Zettabyte to but to say that it would take a whole lot of ones and zeroes to fill it up.

Yottabyte: A Yottabyte is approximately 1,000 Zettabytes. It would take approximately 11 trillion years to download a Yottabyte file from the Internet using high-powered broadband. You can compare it to the World Wide Web as the entire Internet almost takes up about a Yottabyte.

Brontobyte: A Brontobyte is approximately 1,000 Yottabytes. One thing we can say about a Brontobyte is that it is a 1 followed by 27 zeroes.

Geopbyte: A Geopbyte is about 1,000 Brontobytes. One way of looking at a geopbyte is 15267,6504600,2283229,4012496,7031205,376 bytes!

Big Data: getting bigger and bigger, faster and faster

For Big Data applications to be useful, the data needs to be stored, processed and delivered in a comprehensible format so that it can be used effectively. Data volumes are growing very quickly – especially unstructured data – at a rate, typically, of around 50% annually. Josh James, Founder, CEO and Chairman of the Board at Domo, an American computer software company specializing in business intelligence tools and data visualization, recently released their fifth annual *Data Never Sleeps* report, which highlights the fact that 90% of all data today was created in the last two years – that is 2.5 quintillion bytes of data per day.[13]

There are many reasons behind this massive explosion of data. As capabilities of hardware increase and prices decline, the digitization of information becomes cost-effective and sensible from a cost vs. benefit standpoint. The June 2017 report[14] from the Pew Research Center[15] states that about three-quarters of U.S. adults (77%) say they own a smartphone, up from 35% in 2011, making the smartphone one of the most quickly adopted consumer technologies in history. This is natural because as people become more well-off and literate, the appetite for information and the tendency to share increases. Software programming and algorithms are getting better, simpler and easier and hence more complex tasks can be achieved; things which were even unthinkable till a few years ago.

There are several techniques which are available and can be used for Big Data analysis and they are continuously evolving. There are also ready-made software packages available for Big Data and several of them are being used across industries. These technologies can be used to aggregate, manipulate, manage and analyze Big Data. Another emerging and very interesting area is presenting information in such a way that people can use it effectively. This is a key challenge if Big Data is to lead to concrete action. There are human limitations on how much data can be visualized and understood; this increases the relevance of visualization, i.e., techniques and technologies to understand and improve the results of Big Data analyses.

In the next chapter

In this chapter, we looked at the basic characteristics of Big Data and why it is getting larger and more complex with each passing day. We also looked at what is it that makes Big Data different than the data and information which humankind has been using for millennia? We also looked at some of the standard terms which provide us with an idea about the relative size of data and its storage, followed by a discussion of some of the tools that are being used in Big Data Analytics. This was primarily an introduction to what Big Data is all about.

In the next chapter, we discuss the role Big Data is playing in artificial intelligence (AI). It is no exaggeration to say that our ability to store, handle and process huge quanta of data quickly, cheaply and efficiently has played an important role in the development of AI over the last couple of decades. This means that the scientific and technological developments have come together to give AI research a major boost, and at the core of this is data. Data has been a key driver for AI and since the potential of AI is immense in making an indelible impact on societies across the world and on the global economy in the 21st century, Big Data will play an important role in how far AI will go.

Notes

1 Peter Sondergaard is an executive vice president and member of Gartner's operating committee. He leads the company's Research and Advisory organization and he is quoted frequently in the *The New York Times*, *Financial Times*, *The Wall Street Journal*, *The Economist* and CNBC. www.gartner.com/analyst/12/Peter-Sondergaard (accessed on 2nd December 2017).

2 "Top 5 analytics success stories: We take a look at five examples where Big Data has been used successfully" by Simon Barton. https://channels.theinnovationenterprise.com/articles/80-top-5-analytics-success-stories (accessed on 4th December 2017).
   "7 Ways Amazon uses Big Data to stalk you" by Jennifer Wills. www.investopedia.com/articles/insights/090716/7-ways-amazon-uses-big-data-stalk-you-amzn.asp (accessed on 4th December 2017).

3 Definition of "Big Data" in Oxford Dictionaries. https://en.oxforddictionaries.com/definition/big_data (accessed on 7th December 2017).

4 In June 2011, McKinsey Global Institute published a report titled "Big Data: The next frontier for innovation, competition, and productivity," written by James Manyika, Michael Chui, Brad Brown, Jacques Bughin, Richard Dobbs, Charles Roxburgh and Angela Hung Byers. www.mckinsey.com/business-functions/digital-mckinsey/our-insights/big-data-the-next-frontier-for-innovation (accessed on 29th November 2017).

5 "Big Data" by Vangie Beal. www.webopedia.com/TERM/B/big_data.html (accessed on 7th December 2017).

6 "Survey on Big Data," *International Journal of Advanced Research in Basic Engineering Sciences and Technology (IJARBEST)*, by L. Thenmozi and Dr. N. Chandra Kala. www.ijarbest.com/conference/spcl24/1079 (accessed on 15th April 2019).

7 "3D data management: Controlling data volume, velocity and variety". By Doug Laney. https://blogs.gartner.com/doug-laney/files/2012/01/ad949-3D-Data-Management-Controlling-Data-Volume-Velocity-and-Variety.pdf (accessed on 2nd December 2017).

8 "What is Big Data?" in the Gartner IT Glossary. https://web.archive.org/web/20170718161704/https://research.gartner.com/definition-whatis-big-data (accessed on 2nd December 2017).

9 "A formal definition of Big Data based on its essential feature" by Andrea De Mauro, Marco Greco and Michele Grimaldi. www.emeraldinsight.com/doi/full/10.1108/LR-06-2015-0061 (accessed on 2nd December 2017).

10 "Big Data for development: A review of promises and challenges" by Martin Hilbert www.martinhilbert.net/wp-content/uploads/2015/01/BigData4Dev_Hilbert2014.pdf (accessed on 2nd December 2017).

11 "Recent Advances and trends of cyber-physical systems and Big Data analytics in industrial informatics" by Jay Lee, Behrad Bagheri and Hung-An Kao, University of Cincinnati. www.researchgate.net/publication/266375284_Recent_Advances_and_Trends_of_Cyber-Physical_Systems_and_Big_Data_Analytics_in_Industrial_Informatics (accessed on 2nd December 2017).
   "Recent advances and trends in predictive manufacturing systems in big data environment" by Jay Lee, Edzel Lapira, Behrad Bagheri and Hung-an Kao. www.sciencedirect.com/science/article/pii/S2213846313000114 (accessed on 2nd December 2017).

12 "Megabytes, gigabytes, terabytes . . . What are they?" http://whatsabyte.com/ (accessed on 1st December 2017).

13 "Data never sleeps 5.0." https://web-assets.domo.com/blog/wp-content/uploads/2017/07/17_domo_data-never-sleeps-5-01.png (accessed on 2nd December 2017).

14 "10 facts about smartphones as the iPhone turns 10" by Andrew Perrin. www.pewresearch.org/fact-tank/2017/06/28/10-facts-about-smartphones/(accessed on 1st December 2017).

15 The Pew Research Center is a US-based think tank which claims to be non-partisan and carries out research about the issues, attitudes and trends shaping the world. Pew also conducts public-opinion polling, demographic research, content analysis and other data-driven social science research. www.pewresearch.org (accessed on 1st December 2017).

2

BIG DATA AND AI

... what's going to happen is that robots will be able to do everything better than us... I mean all of us. I'm not sure exactly what to do about this. It's really about the scariest problem to me. So I really think we need government regulation here ensuring the public good. You've got companies that have to race to build AI because they're going to be made uncompetitive. If your competitor is racing to build AI and you don't, they will crush you. So they're saying, "We need to build it too . . . . " Transport will be one of the first things to go fully autonomous. But when I say everything, the robots will do everything, bar nothing.

– Elon Musk[1]

Artificial intelligence: how is it different?

The definition of intelligence is highly subjective and there is no consensus over what intelligence really means. It can be defined as the capacity for logic, under-standing, self-awareness, learning, emotional knowledge, planning, creativity and problem-solving. It can be more generally described as the ability or inclination to perceive or deduce information and to retain it as knowledge to be applied towards adaptive behaviors within an environment.[2] Merriam-Webster defines intelligence as the ability to learn or understand things or to deal with new or difficult situations.[3]

Natural intelligence originates in biology. Simply speaking, natural intelligence is how animal or human brains function. But the definition of intelligence which links it to brain alone will be a narrow one as nature also demonstrates non-neural control in plants and protozoa and distributed intelligence in colony species like ants, hyenas and humans.[4] However, for all practical purposes, *human intelligence* is referred to as natural intelligence. Human intelligence or natural intelligence is created naturally and biologically.

This is different from intelligence which is created by humans in machines using technology. It is expected that there will be differences between natural

Natural Intelligence - Complex movements - Tasks with ambiguity - Subjective thinking	Vs.	Artificial Intelligence - Accuracy - Speed - Objective decision-making

FIGURE 2.1   Advantages – Human Intelligence vs. Artificial Intelligence

intelligence and artificially created intelligence.[5] Naturally, artificial intelligence (AI) has significant dominance in many tasks, especially when it comes to monotonous processes. These include speed, objectivity, evolution and cost. In contrast, biological neural networks also have superiority in some qualities, such as handling complex and different tasks and complex movements.

Big Data is at the core of AI

AI research has seen cycles of ebb and flow in terms of the enthusiasm for what it can deliver. But, due to technological breakthroughs and commercial products, that are influencing human lives in very tangible ways, once again hopes are now high. Driverless cars, Siri and Cortana, IBM Watson, deep learning and automated trading have all become household words. What has also led to a boom in its popularity is a democratization of access to Big Data and other technological advancements such as cloud computing and AI tools.

A variety of scientific and technological developments have come together in the new millennium to give AI research a major boost and at the core of it is data. It has become easier to store an ever-increasing amount of data easily and cheaply. The computational resources have become powerful enough, allowing easy access to sieve through this data. Over the last 20 years, our ability to store, analyze and manipulate tremendous amounts of data has increased by leaps and bounds. This has been a key driver for AI.

The need to own and pay for expensive infrastructure to do AI research has decreased considerably with the advent of cloud computing. And a number of mathematical and statistical tools in machine learning have become widely tested and freely available. Access to Big Data, cloud computing and AI-ML (artificial intelligence-machine leaning) has also become democratized, with researchers and companies willing to share information. It is possible, affordable and practical now for a high school student to open an account on Amazon or Google websites and start doing AI-related tinkering. The easy accessibility to Big Data methods can potentially make progress even faster.

While the 1900s saw major advances in AI and computing, the most important advances such as Big Data, responsible for making AI what it is today, took place in the 21st century. As we discuss in several other places in this book, Big Data as a technological innovation depended on many enablers for its progress and there were several advancements which played a role and continue to contribute to its development. But one thing is certain, Big Data is at the heart of everything that is transpiring in AI. As Big Data grows, more interesting breakthroughs in AI might potentially happen in the not-so-distant future.

AI is unlike other technology[6]

Roughly speaking, AI can display aspects of the human brain's cognitive functions. It might even improve and evolve into a more refined version of itself. This is a machine which can *think* independently without the need for human inputs or any external prompting. The machine itself could be a computer, a robot, or a virtual-reality-based platform, or anything else which meets the basic definition that it can perform cognitive functions on its own. One possible way to create AI is to replicate aspects of the human brain, suh as how the human brain thinks, how it reacts to situations and how humans learn, take decisions and react in emergencies.

This means that AI is different from all other previous technologies developed by humans. While all previous technologies were developed by humans to handle a specific task, the holy grail of AI is to artificially replicate and improve on the human brain. It is possible that eventually AI machines will take over many tasks which currently require human intelligence and so this technology will be different from anything else that humankind has ever developed. It is very likely that when AI begins to learn on its own and self-improve without outside intervention, it will eventually maximize its autonomy. This also raises an uncomfortable thought and possibility. If an AI system can continue to improve without any constraints and the system is also autonomous to change and adapt, it might ultimately become independent.

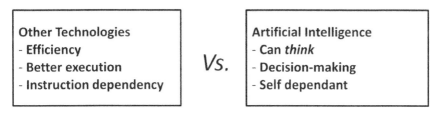

FIGURE 2.2 AI vs. Other Technologies

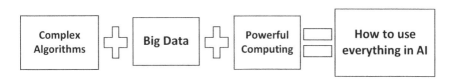

FIGURE 2.3 Big Data – The Characteristics and Processing

AI is driven by four basic characteristics. The first is complex algorithms which attempt to mimic the decision-making process based on multiple inputs and which have multiple optimization variables, including tangible and intangible factors. The second is the ability of algorithms to make use of huge amounts of data, commonly known as Big Data, data which is already available and which is being collected at an ever-increasing rate across the globe. The third is assessing the needs of the required computing capability that can use these algorithms and which has the ability to process this data. These three are different parts of a complex jigsaw puzzle. What makes the picture complete is how these pieces fit together and this is the most difficult and intelligent part.

AI – interaction of many academic disciplines

Although recent attempts to understand the brain may have belonged to the field of biology and medicine, substantial contributions have come from many academic branches. The tools and techniques developed in other areas and theoretical advances in other disciplines have helped in developing a better understanding of the brain and its functioning. So much so that it would be very difficult to claim today that brain studies belong entirely to any one particular academic discipline.

Artificial intelligence is a science focusing on the development of functions similar to human intelligence, such as cognition, reasoning, speech recognition, language skills, learning, problem-solving and the development of emergency responses such as "fight or flight". It is natural that, as a science, it draws from many academic disciplines and calls for expertise in disciplines such as computer science, medicine, biology, psychology, linguistics, mathematics and engineering.

AI is focusing on the development of computer functions which mirror human intelligence, such as cognition, compliance with socially acceptable norms and practices, reasoning, convincing, learning, knowledge transfer and problem-solving.

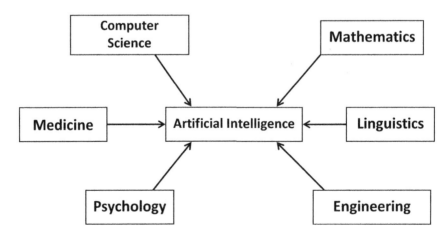

FIGURE 2.4 AI – At the Intersection of Many Academic Disciplines

So, multiple areas can contribute to building an intelligent system: mathematics, biology, philosophy, computer science, sociology and neurology. This list is not exhaustive and it is not unusual for other, less obvious, disciplines to contribute towards AI development. This is one of the important reasons why AI is unique and different from other technologies and why, at times, progress in AI is dependent on advancements in several disciplines.

AI is for decision-making, other technology is about better execution

Throughout human history, the focus of science has been on developing an understanding of natural phenomena and then identifying the laws of nature associated with them. For simple processes, this was done one by one and, for complex ones, in conjunction with many others. Prehistoric man, through trial and error, figured out causal relations: that if X happens, Y will follow. These lessons were later used to make predictive models for things around them. This predictive model could be used to develop useful technologies to make things that reduced human effort and improved their quality of life.

The main focus of science and technology's efforts throughout human history has been to make the lives of human beings easier. The common thread in various technological endeavors has been that humans knew what they wanted and what they wanted to achieve. They were deciding the direction and were trying to figure out "how". They were taking the decisions on what is right and what is wrong, of what is acceptable and what is not. Deciphering nature's laws and then putting limits on usage and practical applications was the path to progress.

In the entire process of scientific and technological achievement, humans have always been in control of "what" they want to achieve and "where" they wanted to reach and "how" they wanted to get there. The philosophy and final objective remained virtually the same behind each and every scientific and technological invention: a safer, better, longer, happier and more comfortable life for humans. The objective has always been to reduce the misery of humankind traditionally brought about by natural phenomena or by human follies.

But AI could be different from all other scientific and technological developments so far. In the case of AI, humans are increasingly letting go of their control on decision-making. Humans are showing faith in machines and trusting non-human intelligence to make decisions on their behalf. Increasingly, these decisions are not just the straightforward and simple ones but also the more subjective ones, the ones which require interpretation, the ones which are ambiguous, and the ones which do not yet have all the information and where the background is fuzzy.

In simpler terms, before AI, we were always in control of the "thinking aspect"; we never outsourced the thinking part to machines. However, this could change with AI. We are outsourcing the thinking part. Other technologies are similar in finding the most optimal path when we have already taken a decision about the direction, but AI is about both: the direction as well as the most optimal path.

This is the key difference between other technologies and AI. In the context of AI, can thinking be outsourced, or, more importantly, *should* thinking be outsourced is the question facing all of us today.

AI handling unstructured challenges

Consider a large hospital where the oncology patients are advised by cancer specialists about diagnosis and the right course of treatment. Human experts usually make the final choice between invasive surgery and non-invasive methods for a particular patient. Human experts can use their experience and judgment when they see a case without precedent in their medical careers. Non-AI machines can only be helpful if a similar case exists in the database. But AI research is fast progressing in the direction where AI-based machines will be able to take decisions just like any other human expert, based on the data and experience.

Most technologies have a specific purpose and are given a predefined problem that needs to be solved. The task or the problem could be as mundane as doing tricky mathematical calculations or as complex as flying an aircraft and making weather forecasts. However, irrespective of the situation, technological advancements have a predefined and well-articulated purpose, function and cost. A machine, a simulation or a computer program can answer the specific questions and handle the problems it is meant to solve. In most cases, scientific discovery and innovation has followed a linear path where the solution may have been invisible, but the problem was visible and definable. Even if the path was not known, the starting point and destination were usually visible to researchers.

The case of AI is different. Apart from solving simple or complex, well-defined problems and doing specific tasks, machines with AI can also answer unstructured and generic questions in their area of expertise. The objective and response mechanism for an AI machine doesn't always need to be predefined and could even fall outside the realm of possibilities imagined at the time of its design. Non-AI programs and machines would only be able to handle the situations for which they have been programmed and that they are familiar with. However, in principle, AI-based machines would not have this constraint.

We may not have all the answers but AI is different and disruptive

Today, we don't have all the answers. But there is no doubt that AI is a disruptive force and it certainly has the potential to become a powerful game changer. We understand that "disruptive" or "disruption" is a much-abused word today, especially in the area of technology. However, AI technology has already proved that there are times when it is disruptive in a real sense. Ask the bricks-and-mortar stores about Amazon or the licensed taxi drivers about Uber.

Supporters of AI claim that these concerns are unfounded because doomsday scenarios have been proven wrong umpteen times in the course of history. The tractor was supposed to render thousands of workers jobless, the automobile was a threat for drivers of horse carriages and, similarly, thousands of people were supposed to lose their jobs when computers came on the horizon. However, millions of new jobs were created and humankind witnessed the advent of several new industries whenever these changes happened.

The change is already visible. A number of smart-home devices now use some basic form of AI. By setting defaults and preferences, indoor lighting might adjust depending on where you are and what you are doing. Siri and Google Voice can understand instructions and follow them. Recommendation systems in Netflix or Pandora can learn your preferences from your previous choices and make good recommendations for movies or music. News-writing bots can now write simple reporting pieces at news agencies such as AP, Yahoo and Fox.[7] You might be getting help from an online customer support member at your favorite website without even realizing that the helper is really an AI bot. Fraud detection, purchase prediction, smart cars, the list goes on. Change is ubiquitous, though we may not always notice it when it is continuous and slow.

The shift from real to virtual and the impact on psychological health

In an interesting paper[8] titled "Prevalence of perceived stress, symptoms of depression and sleep disturbances in relation to Information and Communication Technology (ICT) use among young adults – an explorative prospective study," researchers looked at whether a high quantity of ICT-use is a risk factor for developing psychological symptoms among young users. A group of college students was assessed on different types of ICT-use and perceived stress, symptoms of depression and sleep disturbances.

This paper also suggests that, for women, a high combined use of computer and mobile phone was associated with reports of an increased risk of prolonged stress and symptoms of depression; also, an increased number of text messages per day was associated with prolonged stress. Online chatting was also associated with prolonged stress and emailing and online chatting were associated with symptoms of depression, while Internet surfing was shown to increase the risk of developing sleep disturbances. These findings clearly suggest that ICT may have an impact on psychological health.

There is more evidence. Another research paper,[9] "Association between media use in adolescence and depression in young adulthood – a longitudinal study," highlights the association between media exposure and depression. The objective of the study was to assess the longitudinal association between media exposure in adolescence and depression in young adulthood in a nationally representative sample. The study found that people with more media exposure had significantly greater odds of developing depression. The conclusion was that television exposure and total media exposure in adolescence are associated with increased odds of depressive symptoms in young adulthood, especially in young men.

There are also more localized studies. In further research,[10] "A prospective study of screen time in adolescence and depression symptoms in young adulthood," the researchers examine the association between screen time in adolescence and depressive symptoms in young adulthood among Danish adolescents. It was found that limiting screen time, particularly television viewing, during adolescence may be important for preventing depression in young adulthood. This was an important finding because only when you are able to establish a definite link between habits or behavior and mental health issues, will you be able to take pre-emptive action.

In "Association between screen time and depression among US adults,"[11] surveys conducted into general populations found that the prevalence of depression is about 9% in the United States. The objective of this study was to assess the relationship between television watching/computer use and depression. In this study, depression was found to be significantly higher among females and the results showed that moderate or severe depression levels were associated with higher time spent on TV watching and use of computers. The study concluded that TV watching and computer use can predict depression levels among adults.

Just like the impact of television, smartphones, the Internet and other technologies such as virtual reality, there is a very high likelihood that AI, by its nature, will lead to a deep psychological impact on newer generations. Whether AI will be good or bad for us and how good or how bad it will be, only time will tell. But this is an important dimension of AI which will have significant social implications. It would help to sensitive about these issues and to try and see them in totality without being in a hurry to declare AI as simply good or bad.

Whether the new developments in AI will create more inequalities between societies and countries, leading to more discord, or whether they will lead to more prosperity and peace, depends on what we do today. It is likely that the stakeholders will feel obliged to behave responsibly if the discussion on AI becomes prominent in mainstream culture and if the role of AI takes center stage in frontline media. The issue has been sidelined for some time, but we cannot postpone fully addressing the questions any longer. The public has to get involved and opinion-makers have a big role to play in this.

In the next chapter

In this chapter, we discussed how Big Data was one of the key drivers for AI and how advances in Big Data are intricately linked with developments in AI. This is important because AI is a disruptive force and it certainly has the potential to become a powerful game changer. AI technology has already proved that there are several industries in which AI is bringing about irreversible changes. The debate on how beneficial the influence of AI is, or who will benefit and who will lose out will continue, but it is absolutely certain that AI is here to stay.

In the next chapter, we discuss the difference in approach between Big Data and conventional statistical modeling methods. Big Data analytics and its inferences are based on inductive reasoning, unlike most other mathematical deductions which are based on a deductive approach. This is one of the key differences, which leads to another important problem: the lack of perfect answers and less-than-precise inferences. This does not mean that Big Data is not useful, but we need to be sensitive to the fact that, just like other tools, it too has limitations and we need to treat them with respect.

We will also discuss how Big Data is prone to misuse when the intentions behind it are not completely honest and there is a lack of total transparency in what data we are using and what inferences users of Big Data are trying to draw. The insights and correlations derived from Big Data are dependent not only on the method of analysis but also on the fact of whether there is an agenda behind the patterns one is looking for. Data can't speak for itself, hence it could be prone to manipulation and misuse[12] and this is the theme of the next chapter.

Notes

1 "Top Big Data, AI, and HPC quotes of 2017" by Doug Black. www.datanami.com/2017/12/21/top-big-data-ai-hpc-quotes-2017 (accessed on 9th March 2018).
    Elon Musk is a South African-born Canadian-American businessman, investor, engineer and inventor. Musk is known for his unconventional, courageous ideas. He is the founder, CEO, and CTO of SpaceX; co-founder, CEO, and product architect of Tesla Inc.; co-founder and chairman of SolarCity; co-chairman of OpenAI; co-founder of Zip2; and founder of X.com, which merged with Confinity and took the name PayPal. www.forbes.com/profile/elon-musk (accessed on 15th April 2019); www.tesla.com/elon-musk (accessed on 15th April 2019).
2 "Thoughts on AI from a psychological perspective: Defining intelligence" by T. Panova. http://psybertronic.com/thoughts_on_ai_from_a_psychological_perspective (accessed on 15th April 2019).
3 Definition of "Intelligence" from *Merriam-Webster Dictionary*. www.learnersdictionary.com/definition/intelligence (accessed on 23rd October 2017).
4 "Natural intelligence (NI) is the opposite of artificial intelligence: it is all the systems of control that are not artefacts, but rather are present in biology. Normally when we think of NI we think about how animal or human brains function, but there is more to natural intelligence than neuroscience. Nature also demonstrates non-neural control in plants and protozoa, as well as distributed intelligence in colony species like ants, hyenas and humans. Our behaviour co-evolves with the rest of our bodies, and in response to our changing environment. Understanding natural intelligence requires understanding all of these influences on behaviour, and their interactions." from "Understanding natural intelligence" by Joanna Bryson. www.cs.bath.ac.uk/~jjb/web/uni.html (accessed on 23rd October 2017).
5 From comments by Egor Dezhic, AI and CogSci enthusiast and author of CognitiveChaos.com at *Becoming Human: Artificial Intelligence Magazine*. https://becominghuman.ai/artificial-vs-natural-intelligence-626b6c7addb2 (accessed on 24th October 2017).
6 *Artificial Intelligence: Evolution, Ethics and Public Policy* by Saswat Sarangi and Pankaj Sharma (2019, Abingdon, Oxon: Routledge).
7 "This News-writing bot is now free for everyone" by Klint Finley. www.wired.com/2015/10/this-news-writing-bot-is-now-free-for-everyone (accessed on 20th November 2017).
8 "Prevalence of perceived stress, symptoms of depression and sleep disturbances in relation to information and communication technology (ICT) use among young adults – An explorative prospective study" by Sara Thomée, Mats Eklöf, Ewa Gustafsson, Ralph Nilsson, Mats Hagberg. https://doi.org/10.1016/j.chb.2004.12.007. *Computers*

in Human Behavior, (Volume 23, Issue 3). www.sciencedirect.com/science/article/pii/ S0747563204002250 (accessed on 25th January 2018).

9 "Association between media use in adolescence and depression in young adulthood – A longitudinal study" by Brian A. Primack, Brandi Swanier, Anna M. Georgiopoulos, Stephanie R. Land, and Michael J. Fine. www.ncbi.nlm.nih.gov/pmc/articles/PMC300 4674/?iframe=true&width=100%25&height=100%25 (accessed on 25th January 2018).

10 "A prospective study of screen time in adolescence and depression symptoms in young adulthood" by A. Grøntved, J. Singhammer, K. Froberg, N.C. Møller, A. Pan, K.A. Pfeiffer, and P.L. Kristensen. www.ncbi.nlm.nih.gov/pubmed/26303369 (accessed on 25th January 2018).

11 "Association between screen time and depression among US adults" by K.C Madhav, S. P. Sherchand, and S. Sherchan. www.ncbi.nlm.nih.gov/pubmed/28879072 (accessed on 25th January 2018).

12 "Big-data algorithms are manipulating us all" by Cathy O'Neil in *Wired*, 18th October 2016. Mathematician Cathy O'Neil is also the author of *Weapons Of Math Destruction: How Big Data Increases Inequality and Threatens Democracy*. www.wired.com/2016/10/ big-data-algorithms-manipulating-us (accessed on 26th February 2018).

3

WHAT BIG DATA IS NOT

Listening to the data is important. . . but so is experience and intuition. After all, what is intuition at its best but large amounts of data of all kinds filtered through a human brain rather than a math model?

– *Steve Lohr*[1]

Facebook: connecting the world or in the business of data?[2]

Facebook's unrelenting use of analytics has been one of the most prominent examples of Big Data's potential to be overly intrusive. Their business model is built entirely around the extraction of user data. Their data analysis has been the pillar of Facebook's success. Because of its size and users' addiction, no other platform has as much personal data about its users as Facebook has. Maybe much more than users are comfortable about sharing with a social media platform. Facebook is the world's most popular social media network and it has more than two billion monthly active users worldwide. Because of its extensive reach, as reflected in the number of users it has, Facebook stores enormous amounts of user data.

Facebook is one of the most valuable public companies in the world, with a market value in the hundreds of billions of dollars not because it is so profitable but because it has so much data. Facebook knows who our friends are, what we look like, where we are, what we are doing, our likes, our dislikes and so much more. The more users who use Facebook, the more information it amasses. Facebook collects, stores and analyzes this data to determine user behavior. Facebook tracks its users across the web by using tracking cookies. If a user is logged into Facebook and simultaneously browses other websites, Facebook can track the sites they are visiting.

It is possible to predict data accurately on a range of personal attributes that are highly sensitive just by analyzing a Facebook user's "likes." The patterns of Facebook likes can very accurately predict your sexual orientation, satisfaction with life, intelligence, emotional stability, religion, alcohol use, drug use, relationship status, age, gender, race and political views. The political views part is very controversial. Due to this massive goldmine of data, Facebook can monetize the data and its analytics via advertisers and it is hardly a surprise that Facebook is the most popular social platforms for marketers.

However, this should make a user uncomfortable. Why? Because: (a) does the user know the privacy policies and understand them well? (b) does the user know with whom the data is being shared and in what form? c) does the user know that there could be attempts to influence their opinion by targeting specific information at them? *It is not an exaggeration to say that Facebook is not in the business of connecting the world or facilitating your interactions with your friends, it is in business of data analytics so that it can use the information it has on you.*

Deductive vs. inductive reasoning[3]

In logic, we refer to the two broad methods of reasoning which are *deductive* and *inductive* approaches. It can be argued that Big Data is not a precise science because it is not based on deductive reasoning and works on inductive reasoning. Both these methods are valid but they are conceptually different and hence it is important to understand the difference before we can discuss the suitability and applicability of them.

These two methods of reasoning are characteristically different. Inductive reasoning is open-ended and exploratory and leads to possibilities hitherto unexplored. On the other hand, deductive reasoning is narrow and is only concerned with testing and with confirming or disproving hypotheses. Usually, and most of the time, all practical research involves both inductive and deductive approaches depending on the question under discussion.

Deductive reasoning

Deductive reasoning, or simply deduction, starts with a statement or hypothesis and reaches a specific conclusion.

> In deductive inference, we hold a theory and based on it we make a prediction of its consequences. That is, we predict what the observations should be if the theory were correct. We go from the general – the theory – to the specific – the observations,

said Dr. Sylvia Wassertheil-Smoller, a researcher and professor emerita at the Albert Einstein College of Medicine.[4]

Deductive reasoning usually follows steps. First there is a premise, then a second premise and finally an inference. A common form of deductive reasoning is the syllogism, in which two statements – a major premise and a minor premise – reach a logical conclusion. For example, the premise "Every A is B" could be followed by another premise, "This C is A." Those statements would lead to the conclusion, "This C is B."

Theory > Hypothesis > Observation > Confirmation (Yes or No)

For example, "All computer scientists are hard-working. Tim is a computer scientist. Therefore, Tim is hard-working." For deductive reasoning to be sound, the hypothesis must be correct. It is assumed that the premises, "All computer scientists are hard-working" and "Tim is a computer scientist" are true. Therefore, the conclusion is true. In deductive reasoning, if something is true of a class of things, it is also true for all members of that class. In this case, what applies to Tim because he is a computer scientist will apply to all computer scientists irrespective of other parameters linked to that computer scientist.

Inductive reasoning

Inductive reasoning is the opposite of deductive reasoning and it makes broad generalizations from specific observations, and conclusions are drawn from collected and available data. In arriving at an inductive inference, we make many observations, discern a pattern, make a generalization and propose a theory.

Observation > Pattern > Tentative Hypothesis > Theory

An example of inductive logic is, "The swans in Europe are white. The swans in America are white. The swans in Asia are white. Therefore, all the swans in the world are white." Most readers who have read Nassim Nicholas Taleb[5] will not miss the similarity between this example and the "Black Swan Theory" he has proposed. This is deliberate. In inductive reasoning, the conclusion does not follow logically from the statements.

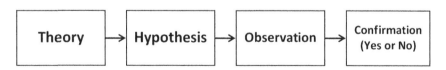

FIGURE 3.1   The Process of Deductive Reasoning

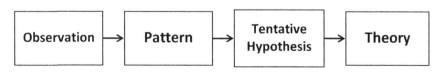

FIGURE 3.2   The Process of Inductive Reasoning

Deduction, induction or a combination of both?

Deductive reasoning is more prevalent when making a forecast on the basis of an available proven theory and this is the basis of scientific experiments and technology. For example, if humans had to travel to the Moon, the laws of physics need to be used to forecast the exact path the spacecraft will take and the time required. The outcome will not change whatever the number of times you conduct a particular experiment. The laws of gravity, of the momentum of conservation, of the conversion of energy, of friction, of air resistance: all of them are proven and they don't change and, once all the calculations have been made correctly without ignoring and omitting a particular influence, the results can be forecast with a high degree of certainty.

However, there are constraints in deductive reasoning because most of the time *we don't know* situations are ambiguous and we don't have a theory available to explain our observations. In these situations, inductive reasoning is commonly used, however the fact remains that it is not always logically valid because it is not always accurate to assume that a general principle is correct based on a limited number of observations, no matter how large that number. For example, if you are tossing a coin and you get ten heads in a row, it doesn't mean that the next time you toss the coin it will land on heads (as long as it is not a trick coin).

Big Data can only offer inductive reasoning

Big Data works by looking at a large set of data followed by pattern recognition and then offering insights and making recommendations. The process uses inductive reasoning and so Big Data is not yet at a stage where it can deliver a 100% foolproof solution. Even if you are interested in employing the services of Big Data, it is not always certain that it will work in a desired and expected manner. Most of the time it is highly likely that Big Data Analytics tools are looking at a situation in a theoretical manner using a purely mathematical approach and therefore the resultant recommendations may turn out to be impractical.

Secondly, the analytics tools are only as good as the data they are using. Moreover, there are times when not everything can be captured in the form of data and not everything that is captured as data will be important. Bruce Cameron, in his 1963 text, "Informal sociology: a casual introduction to sociological thinking" wrote:

> It would be nice if all of the data which sociologists require could be enumerated because then we could run them through IBM machines and draw charts as the economists do. However, not everything that can be counted counts, and not everything that counts can be counted.[6]

More important than the tool is how we use the tool. The problem is not Big Data or Big Data Analytics, the problem is how these tools interact in the ecosystem. People in authority and in responsible positions should be aware that analytics have to be seen in the right context.

Big Data: prone to abuse

We will discuss this issue once again and in detail in Chapter 8 (Big Data: the key questions) and in Chapter 9 (Big Data: is there a question mark on ethics?). However, it is pertinent to touch upon the subject of data abuse here because data analytics is shrouded under so much mystery, that it can be abused equally well as it can be used. Many projects don't reach their logical conclusion in terms of either increasing revenues or reducing costs or, at times, both. Most of the time, executives suffer from tunnel vision as they remain in the comfort zone defined by their areas of industry. With the explosion of digital data led by the Internet boom, better processing power and advanced algorithms, there are many Big Data Analytics firms offering solutions with, at best, mixed results.[7]

Ronald Coase[8] has said "Torture the data, and it will confess to anything." And this remains true with Big Data and Analytics. In an interesting article, "The scary side of Big Data"[9] (21st August 2015), Kate Kochetkova wrote that

> Abuse of Big Data means your worst paranoia scenarios come true, including, among other things, the endless government surveillance, insurance agencies despotism and employers tyranny. Like it or not, the genie is out of the bottle – we've already entered the era of digital spying.

One of the most infamous incidents of abuse involved the company Target when the questionable Big Data practices of a Target store became a talking point.[10] In 2012, a teenage girl bought some pregnancy-related items from a Target store in Minneapolis. Due to Target's aggressive campaign to identify pregnant customers and then recruit them as moms who would buy all of their baby products at Target, the company began sending coupons for diapers and other baby products to the girl's address. The coupons caught the attention of the girl's father, who called the Target store to question why they were sending such coupons to his still-in-high-school daughter. Target knew about the girl's pregnancy before her dad did, which clearly compromised the girl's right to privacy.

In the next chapter

In this chapter we looked at how inductive and deductive reasoning work differently. Because most of the time the pattern and insights seen in Big Data are based on data which has already been accumulated, and users are searching for meaningful information, the reasoning behind it is inductive. It doesn't mean that Big Data inferences will be incorrect but the insights may not always work in practical situations. They are not exactly mathematical formulas and there is a need to be sensitive about the limitations of Big Data. We also looked at the possibility of data abuse in terms of both intention and ethics.

In the next chapter, we look at some of the basic guiding principles of how Big Data works and how we get from a large volume of unstructured information to meaningful and useful insights and then how to convert them into tangible benefits. These principles are not always cast in stone and since most of the time it is an iterative procedure, there are changes and modifications required at each and every step in the analytics process. The development process always has scope for improvement and this is an ongoing exercise.

We also take a look at the need for technical teams and business teams to coordinate and work together. The decisions concerning Big Data (when, data selection, how much, which way, vendor selection, budget, expectations) are all business decisions and managers don't just need to get involved, they also have the final responsibility for these decisions. The data can be analyzed by the best of technical teams but what that data is telling them in the context of their business, only managers can understand. Afterwards, it is only they who can decide how to act on this information.

Notes

1 Steve Lohr has covered technology, business and economics for *The New York Times* for more than 20 years. In 2013, he was part of the team awarded the Pulitzer Prize for Explanatory Reporting. He is the author of *Data-ism* (2015, London: Oneworld) which examines the field of data science and decision-making. He also wrote a history of software and computer programming, *Go To* (2001, New York: Basic Books). www.nytimes. com/by/steve-lohr (accessed on 2nd December 2017).

2 "How Facebook is using Big Data – The good, the bad, and the ugly" by Avantika Monnappa. www.simplilearn.com/how-facebook-is-using-big-data-article (accessed on 17th April 2019).
   "Top 5 analytics success stories" by Simon Barton. https://channels.theinnovation enterprise.com/articles/80-top-5-analytics-success-stories (accessed on 17th April 2019).
   "You are the product" by John Lanchester www.lrb.co.uk/v39/n16/john-lanchester/ you-are-the-product (accessed on 17th April 2019).
   "You are not the Facebook user; you are the product" by Dragos Bratasanu. www. huffingtonpost.com/dragos-bratasanu/you-are-not-the-facebook-user-you-are-the-product_b_7978104.html (accessed on 17th April 2019).

3 "Deductive reasoning vs. inductive reasoning" by Alina Bradford. www.livescience. com/21569-deduction-vs-induction.html (accessed on 17th April 2019).
   "Deduction and induction in social research methods." www.socialresearchmethods. net/kb/dedind.php (accessed on 17th April 2019).
   "Deductive and inductive arguments" from the Internet Encyclopedia of Philosophy. www.iep.utm.edu/ded-ind (accessed on 17th April 2019).
   "Deductive vs. inductive reasoning: Two different approaches to scientific research" by Ashley Crossman.
   www.thoughtco.com/deductive-vs-inductive-reasoning-3026549 (accessed on 17th April 2019).

4 "Deductive reasoning vs. inductive reasoning" by Alina Bradford. www.livescience. com/21569-deduction-vs-induction.html (accessed on 18th April 2019).

5 Nassim Nicholas Taleb is a Lebanese-American essayist, scholar, statistician, former trader, and risk analyst, whose work focuses on problems of randomness, probability, and uncertainty. His book *The Black Swan* (2007, London: Penguin) was described in a review by *The Sunday Times* as one of the 12 most influential books since World War II. The book focuses on the extreme impact of certain kinds of rare and unpredictable events (outliers) and humans' tendency to find simplistic explanations for these events retrospectively. www.fooledbyrandomness.com (accessed on 15th April 2019); https://

fs.blog/nassim-taleb/ (accessed on 15th April 2019); https://fs.blog/2013/08/34-insights-from-nassim-taleb/ (accessed on 15th April 2019). "Stuck in Mediocristan" by Giles Foden (book review). www.theguardian.com/books/2007/may/12/society (accessed on 15th April 2019). *The Black Swan Summary:* "The Black Swan explains why we are so bad at predicting the future, and how unlikely events dramatically change our lives if they do happen, as well as what you can do to become better at expecting the unexpected." https://fourminutebooks.com/the-black-swan-summary (accessed on 15th April 2019).

6 "Not everything that counts can be counted." https://quoteinvestigator.com/2010/05/26/everything-counts-einstein (accessed on 9th December 2017).

7 "Multidisciplinary data science: The view is that since data is everywhere, data science is broadly applicable to all disciplines" by Siddharth Pai. www.livemint.com/Opinion/mkP9m9lVJ638smN0tT5F6J/Multidisciplinary-data-science.html (accessed on 2nd December 2017).

8 Ronald Harry Coase (1910–2013) was a British economist and author. He was the Clifton R. Musser Professor Emeritus of Economics at the University of Chicago Law School, where he arrived in 1964 and remained for the rest of his life. After studying with the University of London External Programme in 1927–29, Coase entered the London School of Economics, where he took courses with Arnold Plant. He received the Nobel Memorial Prize in Economic Sciences in 1991. Coase is best known for two articles in particular: "The nature of the firm" (1937), which introduces the concept of transaction costs to explain the nature and limits of firms, and "The problem of social cost" (1960), which suggests that well-defined property rights could overcome problems of externalities. www.nobelprize.org/prizes/economic-sciences/1991/coase/facts (accessed on 15th April 2019).

9 "The scary side of big data" by Kate Kochetkova. www.kaspersky.com/blog/scary-big-data/9626 (accessed on 9th December 2017).

10 "The use and abuse of Big Data and Hadoop" by Rick Delgado. www.smartdatacollective.com/use-and-abuse-big-datahadoop (accessed on 9th December 2017).

4

HOW DO DATA ANALYTICS WORK?

Without Big Data analytics, companies are blind and deaf, wandering out onto the web like deer on a freeway.

– Geoffrey Moore[1]

Data analytics and German win in 2014 FIFA World Cup[2]

The German Football Association partnered with SAP in order to analyze video data and both individuals' and the team's performance. This allowed them to give individuals feedback on how they can improve their performances and how they could integrate themselves better with one another. SAP is one of the world's most popular enterprise resource-planning (ERP) software products and was developed by the German company SAP SE. Using analytics, the Association cut down average possession time from 3.4 seconds to 1.1 seconds, a critical improvement that made a big difference. The story of how the German Football Association and SAP developed and used "Match Insights" for Germany's competitive advantage is further proof that there is no area where data analytics cannot be used.

Some details about the Match Insights database have been publicly disclosed by the German coaches and SAP executives in press interviews. All of the final 32 teams competing for the World Cup in Brazil had a dedicated performance and video analyst, but Germany was the only one that had a specially built database to measure and analyze individual and team performance and strategies. The German team collected and analyzed a vast amount of data on its own and opposing players.

The data was delivered in a visual and easily understandable manner to its players, trainers and coaches via a custom-built app, so they could use it on their mobile phones or tablets. Developed with input from German national team general manager Oliver Bierhoff, Match Insights was launched in 2012. Each German and each opposing player was assigned a unique identifier, enabling their movements to be tracked digitally and the resulting data used to measure key performance indicators, such as the number of touches, average possession time and movement speeds.

One of the German team's key strategic aims before the World Cup was to improve the speed of its passing. Thanks in part to Match Insights, Germany was able to cut its average possession time and this improvement in possession time enabled the German players to better implement their aggressive, fast-paced style of play. Not only did Germany possess a goldmine of performance data, but it made the data accessible to its users on the right platform with a mobile-first approach. *It would not be an exaggeration to call Match Insights and its data analytics the 12th man of the German team who helped the 11 members play better and contributed to the victory.*

How data analytics works

Data-analytics processes are iterative and most of the time they evolve on an ongoing basis with changes at each and every step. Usually, there is nothing that can be called a typical cycle because specific situations determine which steps will come earlier in the process and whether certain steps will be omitted from the cycle. The following list is neither prescriptive nor exhaustive. However, a sample iterative cycle in data analytics could look something like this:

> **Unstructured Data > Data Capture > Data Sorting > Structured Data > Data Analysis > Actionable Insights > Predictive Models > Future Forecast > Results Evaluation > Process Modifications**

Most of these steps are self-explanatory; however, we think that a brief explanation of each step would not be out of place here:

> **Unstructured Data** – The process begins with unstructured data, which is extremely large in volume. It is like a dump in which you can't really see much pattern and it is even more difficult to see what the data might tell you. For example, a retail chain will be visited by thousands of customers every day and will generate a large number of itemized bills. This is the unstructured data which is large and unmanageable at this point.

> **Data Capture** – The next step in this process is to capture the data that we are going to use from the large, unstructured data that we have. This process can either be selective, in which we leave out some data, or it could be exhaustive, in which we don't really know what to include and what to leave out. For example, an NGO (non-governmental organization), while looking for donors, may decide to leave out certain people on the basis of their annual income. Data capture is the pillar of the whole analytics exercise and there are serious implications for an organization if it goes wrong at this stage. For example, insufficient data will not offer them the right insights and if they are using excessive and unnecessary data, the cost and time taken may increase significantly. If the data capture is not right, nothing else will go right in the value chain.

Data Sorting – After we have selected the data, there is a need to define the variables, which are the basis on which we will sort the data. There are almost infinite combinations possible and we need to select what will work best for us. The data of patients in a hospital can be sorted on the basis of their demographic profile, their professions and income levels, the diseases they have, their dietary habits and whether they have insurance or not, etc. For example, a nutrition expert who is trying to establish a link between alcohol intake and the propensity of a person to develop dementia at a later stage in life will sort the data differently compared to a cardiologist seeing the recurrence of heart diseases and stress levels.

Structured Data – After sorting, we have structured data, which will look much more manageable and clean. This structured data will be qualitatively different from unstructured data. It will be more like a data dump in which things have been sorted and have been put into an orderly form. This dataset will not offer any specific insights but would at least look like it could provide meaningful information if one looks for it more carefully.

Data Analysis – The structured data can be analyzed using several methods, including some of those described in Chapter 1 (Big Data: what, why and how?) This is one of the most critical stages in the value chain, because how you analyze data significantly impacts the quality of insights and inferences. The data analysis will depend on the selection of the correct methods, techniques and execution and these will determine how useful this exercise becomes.

Actionable Insights – Data analysis leads to insights and, at this stage, it is possible that some insights are useful and others may not have any significant use-value. There is a difference between insights and actionable insights. Analytics will throw up insights but some of them will not be useful for an organization. So, while it might be good to be aware of them, they are not of much practical value. For example, the location for a store may not be the most optimal, or regular clientele may not be the best: these variables cannot be changed easily and they also have cost implications, hence such insights are not of great practical value, making them non-actionable. The key here is to look for insights which are actionable and ones where an organization can exercise some control over the variables involved.

Predictive Models – The insights gained will not just be useful in tweaking the processes so that improvements can lead to better results, they can also be used to build predictive models. On the basis of data analysis and insights, technical teams can build predictive models with inputs from business managers. These predictive models may not always be very precise but they would still offer enough clues about the likely impact of the different choices available to business owners or managers. This can be helpful in choosing the most optimal course of action.

Future Forecast – These actionable insights and predictive models can become extremely useful inputs in the business strategy for the future. For example, if a journal subscription service receoves the insight that free gifts are less effective than direct discounts and if it also builds a predictive model which shows that there is a considerable chance of a dip in the number of subscribers, then the business owners may decide to increase discounts and look for diversification in some of the other related areas. Predictive models combined with business strategy could be helpful in generating better future forecasts and decision-making.

Results Evaluation – In both of the following cases: (a) tweaks made on the basis of actionable insights and (b) future forecasts made on the basis of predictive models, the actual results will be compared with expected outcomes. Do results align with expectations or do they miss? If the results are different than those predicted, there is a need to find out why this happened. On the basis of this analysis, more changes and tweaks will be required that might result in the desired outcomes or lead to another round of modifications.

Process Modifications – Irrespective of success or failure at the results-evaluation stage, it is not only possible but highly likely that that the process followed in the development cycle can and should be improved. For example, if an organization had decided to exclude some data at an earlier stage, it may decide to include it now. Or if there were some variables in decision-making which were being analyzed, the number of these variables could be increased or decreased, depending on the end objectives. Organizations may also decide that a certain vendor or a particular technology may not be working that well in the context and they may decide to replace them with new vendors or new technologies which have now become available.

Analytics: the need for business and technology teams to work together

The process discussed in the previous section is presented mainly from the vendor's perspective or the in-house technology team that has been entrusted with the responsibility of building the analytics solutions. However, after we have looked at the important steps which may be a part of the iterative cycle in Big Data analytics, it is pertinent now to look at the important steps in data analytics from an organization's perspective and the core guiding principle which may be helpful in building a more effective analytics solution.

As always, the following is not an exhaustive list and does not cover the specific situations which are relevant for an organization. Nevertheless, it can still work as a roadmap when an organization is starting the process to find the most effective and optimal data-analytics solution for itself.

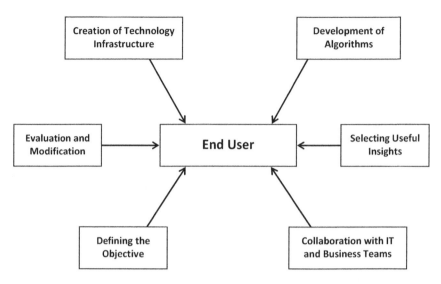

FIGURE 4.1 The End User – Core of the Analytics Process

(1) "The end user" is the core of the analytics process. At each and every point in the development cycle for analytics, the entire process needs to revolve around the end user. Developing a system that is easy to use is more important than anything else. Inertia is the enemy of even the best of initiatives and this applies to analytics too.

(2) Defining the objective is an iterative procedure but there still needs to be a starting point. Unless you start with a reference of what you want to achieve, the cost–benefit analysis cannot be done reliably. Afterwards, there will be changes but they will only make the exercise more efficient. The costs and timelines should be defined as clearly as possible.

(3) The next step is choosing the most appropriate technology for a Big Data initiative. The organization needs to identify the right database software and analytics tools and needs to have the correct technology infrastructure in place. How the project's business goals can be best achieved is essential to zeroing in on the analytics required.

(4) Big Data analytics doesn't mean that all the data an organization has will be put to use. There is a need to separate data that will lead to useful and implementable insights. At times, there will also be the need for an explicitly stated objective or clearly defined question..

(5) The Big Data professionals need to create the algorithms required to generate the desired outputs. Here, the project teams need to continuously communicate with the frontline teams. Better communication and collaboration mean a smoother and faster analytics-development process.

(6) In the development phase, the business teams or internal IT teams need to continuously evaluate how easy or difficult it will be to maintain and incorporate

the enhancements. Notwithstanding the quality of development work, the process of generating Big Data-analytics solutions requires continuous attention and updates and here the project team will need guidance.

(7) At this stage, it is also important to reassess the technology infrastructure that the organization has opted for. It needs to be able to support an evolving development process. The algorithms and development should not be so complicated that they act as a reason for users to dump the infrastructure and move on at the first available opportunity.

Data analytics – it can't replace the domain experts

There is never a 100% guarantee that Big Data analytics will always succeed. But a reasonable set of ground rules can help in increasing the probability of making Big Data initiatives more successful and more effective. The technical factors and the business reasons are equally important drivers in the process. In an interesting article titled "Why data science is simply the new astrology"[3] in the Indian business newspaper *Mint*, Karthik Shashidhar wrote that one of the biggest challenges with data analytics is that many data scientists accept the model that gives the best results on the dataset at hand; no attempt is made to understand why the given inputs lead to the output.

The article says that, essentially, data analytics is an exercise in pattern recognition and, in simple terms, it means that, given a set of inputs and outputs, the system tries to arrive at a mathematical formula such that the outputs can be predicted with as fair a degree of accuracy as possible, given the inputs. The algorithms can also recognize patterns that are not easily visible to the human eye. This works brilliantly in medical science. There is a deep-learning algorithm that performed on par against a team of expert doctors in detecting skin cancer and another algorithm that is able to detect heart arrhythmia by analyzing electrocardiograms, which outperforms the average cardiologist. Similarly, algorithms to detect pneumonia and breast cancer have performed better than experts.

These algorithms are fed with large sets of images that contain both positive and negative cases of the condition to be detected; they calibrate the parameters of a mathematical formula so that patterns that lead to positive and negative cases can be distinguished. Then, when fed with new images, they apply these formulas with the calibrated parameters in order to classify those images. But the trouble is that machines can also go spectacularly wrong. The problem with identifying patterns that are not apparent or intuitive to humans is that meaningless patterns can get picked up and amplified as well. In the statistics world, these are known as "spurious correlations."

To eliminate spurious correlations, statisticians inspect their models with the help of domain experts to make sure that they make "intuitive sense." In case the patterns don't make sense, the models need to be tweaked. However, modern algorithms and models are hard to inspect and, as things become more complex, it is increasingly difficult to check that these models and algorithms make intuitive sense.

The way a large number of data scientists approach a problem is to take a dataset and then apply all possible machine-learning methods to it. They then accept the model that gives the best results on the dataset at hand. No attempt is made to understand why the given inputs lead to the output, or if the patterns make "physical sense."

We think that this article raises an important and extremely relevant question about the use of data and analytics. Unless the entire process of data, algorithms and derived insights is understood well enough – and data scientists are clearly able to establish the linkage between input and output without influencing the systems with their biases and without having an already defined picture of what an optimal output will look like – Big Data may remain prone to misuse and as dangerous as any other technology which could be abused by practitioners. Another dimension is that data experts need to work closely with domain experts so that the conclusions make sense intuitively. Any compromise on this core premise could harm the growth and utility of Big Data immensely.

Big Data analysis of future thinking and decision-making

In a research paper titled "A Big Data analysis of the relationship between future thinking and decision-making," in *PNAS* (Proceedings of the National Academy of Sciences of the United State of America, February 2018), Robert Thorstad and Phillip Wolff discussed that how people think about the future can affect their decisions.[4] The results of the analysis suggest that individuals who think far into the future make a variety of appropriately oriented decisions, such as investing in the future and avoiding future harms. The results also suggest that future thinking may affect decisions by making the future seem more connected to the present.

More broadly, the results from the research show the viability of using automated analyses of social-media texts to measure psychological constructs. Automated analyses of social media are naturalistic – increasing sensitivity to a range of future events and this could mean presenting them in such a way that the sensitivity to a particular range of events increases disproportionately – unsolicited – reducing the effects of experimenter prompting and providing hints about something – and scalable to millions of tweets generated by tens of thousands of individuals. The authors use Big Data methods to investigate how decision-making might depend on future sightedness (that is, on how far into the future people's thoughts about the future extend).

The researchers were able to establish a link between future thinking and decision-making at the population level in showing that US states with citizens having relatively far-future sightedness, as reflected in their tweets, take fewer risks than citizens in states having relatively near-future sightedness. In another study, the researchers analyze people's tweets to confirm a connection between future sightedness and decision-making at the individual level, showing that people with far-future sightedness are more likely to choose larger future rewards over smaller immediate rewards.

It has been shown that risk-taking decreases with increases in future sightedness, as reflected in people's tweets. The ability of future sightedness to predict decisions suggests that future sightedness is a relatively stable cognitive characteristic and this implication was supported in an analysis of tweets by over 38,000 people. The researchers also provide evidence for a potential mechanism by which future sightedness can affect decisions, showing that far-future sightedness can make the future seem more connected to the present, as reflected in how people refer to the present, past and future in their tweets.

We think it is interesting that researchers have been able to conduct a study with the help of new technology on a subject which we intuitively think makes a lot of sense. How we view and imagine the consequences of our decisions today and their implications for our future, plays an important role in influencing how sensible our behavior should be. This also indicates that sometimes technology can make provide scientific explanations for things which are usually considered to be in the domain of the intangible. There is huge utility in data analytics for social issues and for analyzing the behavioral patterns of people. However, the biggest factor always remains: how these insights are interpreted and how the data is viewed.

The role of decision makers in interpreting data

Hidden in a huge mass of data there are clear patterns and if we could read and understand this data properly, we could arrive at actionable business insights.[5] However, are there enough examples to validate that raw data becomes information that turns into wisdom, followed by actionable insights that finally play an instrumental role in value creation? If we want to understand and interpret large data, the datasets must first be made manageable. After that, even if we (users as a whole) gain insights, it may not be that these alone are enough for us to change our business strategy in such a way that it adds value. The data is only there to assist in business decisions, but it is the managers who will make these calls and the quality of these calls is dependent on the interpretation of this data.

For example, very simplistically speaking, if for a retail chain the data says that their upmarket stores do better business on a rent-adjusted basis than their suburban counterparts, does this mean that the company should close down its suburban stores and open more upmarket stores? Not always. Because it is possible that the market in upmarket areas is already saturated and a new store may cannibalize the sales from

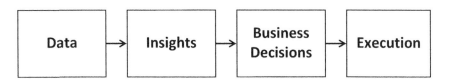

FIGURE 4.2   The Buck Stops with the Business Manager

an existing store in such an area. Also, if the company finds out that the 25–35 age group is usually more demanding but more profitable, does that mean that the company should deploy more resources to take care of this age group? Ultimately, these are business decisions.

The predictive algorithms using Big Data analytics don't need to understand the cause and effect behind statistical relationships. And that is both good and bad. It is good because algorithms do not have the biases which are so common in human judgment. But it is bad because algorithms cannot understand the "why" part and can't empathize with the decision-making process in the way that a human observer can. Too much reliance on these algorithms will take away our power to take the correct course until it is just too late.

In the next chapter

In this chapter, we looked at a typical process in Big Data both from a technical perspective and also from a business perspective. Big Data decision-making processes undergo transformations on a very regular basis and modifications are an integral part of the entire value chain. This is an evolutionary process where it is very difficult to define what "a perfect outcome" or "a perfect process" means. If we use the analogy of a football game: the rules of the game, the goalposts, which 11 players of the squad to field and even the match venue keep shifting, making this an iterative process.

In the next chapter we discuss some of the applications of Big Data. There are several areas where Big Data is making an impact and these include: retail, healthcare, education, government, disaster recovery, politics and election campaigns. It suffices to say that there are hardly any areas that Big Data has not reached or is not making an impact. Of course it is possible that there is a certain amount of hype associated with Big Data and this is natural with any new technology. But to say that it is only hype and no substance would be completely incorrect.

Notes

1 Geoffrey Moore is an American organizational theorist, management consultant and author. He is well known for his work *Crossing the Chasm: Marketing and Selling High-Tech Products to Mainstream Customers* (2014, NewYork: HarperBusiness). Prior to working with the McKenna Group, Moore was a sales and marketing executive at Rand Information Systems, Enhansys and Mitem. https://digitalfullpotential.com/geoffrey-moore-quote-big-data (accessed on 15th April 2019); www.geoffreyamoore.com (accessed on 15th April 2019).

2 "How Big Data helped Germany win the World Cup" by PhocusWire. www.tnooz.com/article/big-data-germany-world-cup (accessed on 4th December 2017).

"Germany's secret World Cup weapon: Big Data" by Jack Rosenberger. www.cioinsight.com/it-news-trends/germanys-secret-world-cup-weapon-big-data.html (accessed on 4th December 2017).

"Top 5 analytics success stories" by Simon Barton. https://channels.theinnovation enterprise.com/articles/80-top-5-analytics-success-stories (accessed on 17th April 2019).

"Athletes to analysts: How Big Data gave the German football team a leg up" by Saheli Roy Choudhury.

www.cnbc.com/2016/07/07/euro-2016-sap-and-german-football-team-worked-to-develop-big-data-analytics.html (accessed on 4th December 2017).

3 "Why data science is simply the new astrology" by Karthik Shashidhar. *Mint* newspaper, www.livemint.com/Sundayapp/zDSjhU5IzcuI7ypo6W4WtL/Why-data-science-is-simply-the-new-astrology.html (accessed on 25th February 2018).

4 "A Big Data analysis of the relationship between future thinking and decision-making" by Robert Thorstad and Phillip Wolff. www.pnas.org/content/115/8/E1740.short?rss=1 (accessed on 25th February 2018); www.pnas.org/content/115/8/E1740.full (accessed on 25th February 2018); www.pnas.org/content/115/8/E1740/tab-article-info (accessed on 25th February 2018).

5 "Why the promise of big data hasn't delivered yet" by Rosemary Barnett. https://techcrunch.com/2017/01/29/why-the-promise-of-big-data-hasnt-delivered-yet (accessed on 3rd December 2017).

5

BIG DATA

The applications

If we have data, let's look at data. If all we have are opinions, let's go with mine.
– *Jim Barksdale*[1]

Big Data Analytics and "the human genome"

Over the last few years, Big Data has played a key role in decoding information hidden in human genes.[2] Genomics is the study of the complete genetic material (genome) of organisms. The stream includes sequencing, mapping and analyzing a wide range of RNA and DNA codes, from viruses and mitochondria to many species across the kingdoms of life. There are intensive efforts to determine the entire DNA sequence of many individual humans in order to map and analyze individual genes as well as their interactions. To be clear, genomics is not a brand new pursuit, since genes have been studied and mapped for decades. However, Big Data analytics are helping researchers and scientists to make further progress on the human genome.

In fact, Big Data and analytics are tailor-made for research in genetics because genes contain enormous amounts of information which could not be studied so efficiently otherwise. The amount of data being produced by sequencing, mapping and analyzing genomes is huge. Each human genome has 20,000–25,000 genes, comprised of three million base pairs. This amounts to 100 gigabytes of data. Sequencing multiple human genomes would quickly add up to hundreds of petabytes of data and the data created by the analysis of gene interactions multiplies this even further.

There are specific and more significant achievements of Big Data analytics as well. With the help of Big Data, scientists have been able to observe the "social character" of genes. Scientists wanted to figure out the inner workings of the complex genetic effects that take part in the creation of complex diseases. This goal had been particularly difficult because genetic expressions of certain diseases usually come from the combination of several genetic markers that interact with each other. Now, scientists have been able to address this challenge using statistical tools from Big Data analytics.

By studying the data from a human genome, scientists can create more effective and appropriate treatments for patients. A generic approach can be replaced with an approach that works best with each individual person. This not only results in better outcomes but can also result in less time being needed for treatment. Big Data analytics can also help in creating health records, which are stored and accessed by doctors. Based on the analysis of genes, doctors are able to identify heritable traits that can be passed on to the next generation.

The cost part of this is another dimension. By the time the Human Genome Project was completed in April 2003, the cost of sequencing the human genome was $40 million, down from $95 million just two years before. Now, Big Data is helping to make sequencing more affordable. Today an individual human genome can be sequenced for around $5,000 consistently and accurately and the next exciting challenge companies are working with is to bring this cost down to $1,000. *Increasingly, Big Data will make significant contribution in saving human lives and making the quality of healthcare which is better but available at cheaper prices.*

Big Data is revolutionizing the retail industry

Big Data technology is beneficial for: (1) targeted offers and deals for individual customers, (2) demand forecast and supply-chain efficiency and (3) more effective handling of loyalty programs. In-depth knowledge of customer behavior, preferences and habits are important for making better pitches to them. Targeted campaigns can be devised so that funds can be used more efficiently.

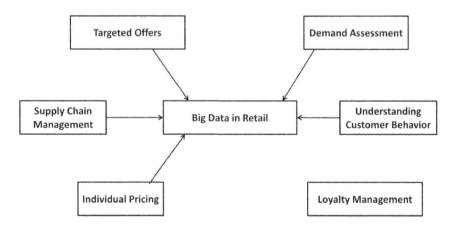

FIGURE 5.1 Retail – Big Data and its Impact

Knowing the customer

It is vital for businesses to understand how much customers matter, as in how important they are for their business[3] in respect to top-line and bottom-line contributions, good or bad word of mouth, how loyal they are and how sustainable their contribution will be. The following examples contain broad generalizations but still help to explain this better:

- If as a business you are focused on the top line, someone who is buying lot of high-value products is more valuable than someone buying fewer. This is a simple deduction and can be assessed depending on what, as an organization, you are looking for: for example bottom-line, offline, or online purchases; recurring small purchases, or bulk purchases, etc.
- How strongly does the customer advocate your products or services? For example, someone buying more from you and contributing higher in revenue and profitability may seem more important but, in reality, this customer is much less valuable for you than someone else who may not be buying that much directly but who is very effective in spreading good word of mouth about you, thereby significantly helping you to attract more customers.
- If all other parameters are similar, someone who is 70 years old, or who is staying in this (key business) location for only a short while, is less valuable for you than someone who is 30 years old or a permanent resident in this location. Of course, the permanent vs. temporary distinction will be much less applicable for online businesses and e-commerce activities.
- There could be other parameters as well. For example, how proactive the customer is in sharing feedback and how useful customer feedback is in making your products and services better.

There are several possible data points including location, age, past behavior, interests, activity time, brand interaction, purchasing power, habits and more. The data will help you in more effective and personalized marketing plans, which could contribute to the growth in profitability and revenue of your business. Everything we have spoken about here depends on how much you know bout your customers and that requires that you collect as much information about them as possible. This will help you to understand the worth of a customer better and also to produce more actionable insights into customer behavior. The more customer data and the more analysis of collected data you have, the better your understanding of them will be.

Big Data is the key to affordable, quality healthcare

Big Data can be used to recommend preventive treatment as doctors can analyze and use a patient's characteristics to predict the risk of them acquiring chronic conditions. This will not only ensure early intervention but will also reduce the costs of healthcare needs. This data, which is useful for an individual patient, can also be pooled and used to predict trends for a defined set of the population to estimate future healthcare needs.[4]

Case Study: India and its aging-related diseases[5]

In Srinivasapura, Karnataka, the Centre for Brain Research (CBR), which is part of the Indian Institute of Science (IISc) – the premier institution for scientific research in India – is collecting time-series data to help predict aging-related disorders early. This is important, as the demographics will soon undergo a change. For example, two-thirds of 1.3 billion Indians are younger than 35 but UN data projects that one in six Indians will be older than 60 by 2050; this figure was one in 20 about 25 years ago. India has 2.4% of the world's land mass and more than 17% of its population. By the year 2020, the country will account for 14.2% of the world's 60+ year-olds. By the end of this century, the elderly will constitute more than one-third of the Indian population, up from 8% in 2015 and 19% in 2050.

In developed countries, approximately 10% of people over 65 years old have dementia. CBR says

> The prevalence doubles every five years after the age of 60 and reaches nearly 50% after the age of 85 years. An estimated 35.6 million people worldwide were living with dementia in 2010 . . . . The numbers in developed countries are forecast to increase by 100% between 2001 and 2040 on average, but by more than 300% in India.

There are more risk factors for the Indian population, such as hypertension, diabetes, obesity, smoking and alcohol abuse.

India, already handicapped with an anemic health budget, is ill-equipped to handle the ballooning of its elderly population and the mental health issues that accompany it. The premise and promise of the Srinivasapura Ageing Senescence and Cognition (SANSCOG) project are that it could, eventually, potentially help develop drugs more suited for Indian conditions and genetic makeup. Drugs developed in the Western world and sold in India are pricey and may not be effective for Indian genes.

All the medical data captured from 10,000 people will be first stored in an Android app developed by the CBR team at IISc. The data collected by field agents and volunteers over the year will be channeled to a central supercomputing server at IISc. And this is where the data sets will start getting bigger and more complex. For instance, each individual's data could go up to a few terabytes in size. Genetic data alone can be as big as 2 terabytes per person. MRI data can be as high as 200 gigabytes depending how much processing is done.

With each individual's data running into a few terabytes, the total storage required will surely be in petabytes. By sifting through petabytes of datasets over

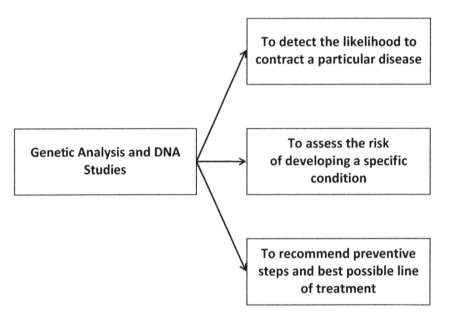

FIGURE 5.2 Data Analytics in Healthcare

the next few years, the aim is to build models and develop software algorithms, which will help predict the onset of brain-related diseases early enough. Conditions such as Alzheimer's, diabetes, liver disorders, obesity and others have a particular genetic component to them. Without its own genomic database, India has been lagging behind. CBR and the Genome India project will ensure there is India-specific Big Data available for advanced research.

The personalized information about an individual, including his or her genetic analysis is already being used to detect the likelihood of contracting a disease and the risks for specific conditions. With the help of this data, people can take preventive steps to avoid the kinds of behavior which might increase their risks of such. There are already molecular diagnostics companies which are doing this in order to make people more aware about their health. These companies offer personalized recommendations based on genetic tests and diagnoses. This is a big enhancement in preventive healthcare.

Big Data has tremendous potential for automating processes and reducing workloads for doctors and support staff so that they can focus on more critical challenges. Better data and better analyses of the accumulated and available data enable healthcare professionals to reduce the chances of making mistakes. All of this can reduce costs and improve the accessibility of the best possible, quality healthcare for poor and remote populations.

Big Data can also help with faster and more accurate diagnoses of rare diseases. If a rare disease is diagnosed, it is very likely that there is very little data about this disease available for researchers. Hence it is important that whatever data is available, in any part of the world, is available for researchers and that is where Big Data can be extremely helpful. If researchers have online access to a large database which contains previous instances of diseases and all other relevant information, it will help in understanding rare diseases quickly, so that treatments can be tried.[6]

There are other applications in healthcare too. For example, AI diagnoses of eye diseases, using Big Data analyses, such as for macular degeneration and diabetic macular edema can be achieved by viewing non-invasive light-based optical coherence tomography (OCT) scans. The AI can also make referral and treatment recommendations. Macular degeneration and diabetic macular edema are the two most common causes of irreversible blindness but they are treatable if detected early. If Big Data and AI tools can be used to detect them, this can have a very positive impact on treating these diseases.[7]

The same method can be applied to chest X-rays of childhood pneumonia, where computers are able to determine the difference between viral and bacterial pneumonia with greater than 90% accuracy. The distinction between viral and bacterial pneumonia is key for deciding the course of treatment. Viral pneumonia is treated mainly with supportive care, while bacterial pneumonia can be treated with antibiotics. This technology could have other potential applications, such as distinguishing between cancerous and non-cancerous lesions in CT scans or MRIs. This data and these tools have been made open-source so that other groups can use them.[8]

Big Data can help governments and authorities

Many governments and authorities with good intentions and who want to be accountable are already (and if not, they will be soon) using data to measure everything. Once they have a good handle on data capture and analysis, they are able to set goals and compare results and accomplishments against expectations or targets. There are already several governments and administrative bodies using data to devise better policies and a more effective response from administrations. The interesting part is that the scope for improvement by using Big Data is much higher in places where inefficiencies in the system are also high. If processes are

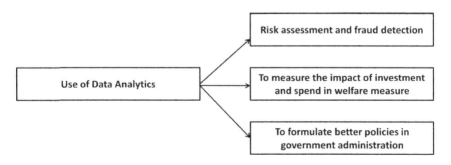

FIGURE 5.3 Data Analytics in Government and Administration

streamlined, more data is captured in an efficient manner and this data can then be used to devise better policies without bias. Some of the developing countries in Asia and Africa can benefit from this much more than developed countries.

Are central banks relying on more and better data to make policies?

Benoît Cœuré, member of the Executive Board of the European Central Bank (ECB), at the conference on Economic and Financial Regulation in the Era of Big Data, organized by the Banque de France (Paris, 24th November 2017), admitted that in crunch situations, traditional statistical datasets and the models used by administrative bodies proved inadequate to support the decision-making process, meaning that there is a need to obtain timelier and richer data for policy analysis.[9] Policymakers today have access to a large number of micro-datasets, often very different in nature and scope. Some are the result of new regulations and others are by-products of the increased use of technology. However, if used appropriately and responsibly, they can help policymakers to extract more timely and diverse economic signals and thus they are a meaningful complement to existing official data.

There are areas in which central banks have started collecting large amounts of data to help them monitor developments in financial markets and allow them to extract richer information about the transmission of monetary policy. This in turn helps to calibrate policies. The money-market statistical-reporting (MMSR) data, has been collected, since July 2016, by the European Central Bank in collaboration with the wider Eurosystem. MMSR data contain confidential daily information on the individual euro-denominated loans in the euro money market from the 52 largest euro-area banks, which collectively account for approximately 80–85% of the total balance sheet of euro-area banks.

At present, this means collecting information on 10,000 daily transactions in the unsecured money market, with a daily volume of around €100 billion. The system also collects data on around 30,000 daily transactions on secured loans, worth around €500 billion. The high volume of data, combined with the high frequency with which it is collected, means that the standard verification process involving human beings is not feasible. Carrying out checks by algorithm, using machine-learning techniques and artificial intelligence is one way of ensuring that data remain of high quality.

Central banks have made considerable progress in integrating big new datasets into their policy analyses and decision-making. Granular data collected by central banks themselves have, in particular, become an indispensable source of information for policymakers. Although evidence is growing that online data may provide tangible benefits for short-term forecasting, more research is needed to ensure that the data are of sufficient quality and reliability. The potential of such data to enrich central bank analysis in the future is considerable.

Big Data can take us closer to the goal of poverty alleviation

There are many misconceptions and stereotypes about the lives and choices of the poor. There are several critical issues and decision variables which are important for poor, like food availability, education, size of family, the need for healthcare, risk management, how microcredit can help and to save for the future. Data can offer enough useful insights into what could make the actions of governments and NGOs more effective. Perhaps the most important thing is that we move away from pre-conceived notions about the poor and the consensus view about the causes underlying their poverty.

Though all the experiments conducted locally and the associated data collection, may not be truly representative of what is happening at the macro level, they offer enough insights into how data can be used and analyzed to design better policies. There are important lesson to learn from the work that is already happening in this area: (a) the task of eliminating poverty is not unmanageable if we divide the problem into many smaller parts and tackle them, (b) there is not always a need for big-bang reforms and social revolution and things can actually progress without making sweeping changes and (c) the politics of developing countries and good policies are not always inconsistent.

Data collection and analysis can certainly offer the hope that if we keep evaluating the data and tweaking policies according to the results, it may be possible to eliminate extreme poverty in the future, if not in our lifetime. Because no matter how complex and impossible the problem of poverty looks, it is not entirely unsolvable. Data science can help in providing better access to education, healthcare and financial services for the poor and it can also help to reduce inefficiency by bringing in more transparency. Simply speaking, access to Big Data can help governments and NGOs to work more efficiently and to achieve better results with the same resources.

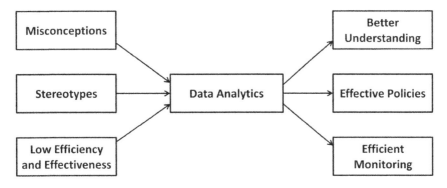

FIGURE 5.4 How Data is Helping in the Alleviation of Poverty

Abdul Latif Jameel Poverty Action Lab (J-PAL)[10]

The Abdul Latif Jameel Poverty Action Lab (J-PAL) is a network of 158 affiliated professors from 51 universities. The mission of J-PAL is to reduce poverty by ensuring that policy is informed by scientific evidence and this is done through research, policy outreach and training across six regional offices worldwide. J-PAL is extensively using data analytics. There are several areas where J-PAL has been at work, using data to compare results and recommend effective policy measures and this includes education, healthcare, violence and crime control, microcredit, finance, agriculture and public policy.

There are several examples of when collected data was used to offer more effective program. For example, in one of its interesting insights, J-PAL proved that cognitive behavioral therapy (CBT) reduced criminal and violent behavior among young men in cities.[11] In Chicago Public Schools in the United States, arrests per student decreased by 12% by the end of the program, with a 20% reduction in arrests for violent crime. In Monrovia, Liberia, CBT deterred an average of 26 crimes per participant in the year following the program. When delivered in schools, CBT also increased graduation rates. In the United States, students who received in-school CBT were 9% more likely to graduate high school on time, even though the reduction in crime among this group did not persist beyond the year-long program.

Disasters can't be prevented but Big Data can help to mitigating the impact

To provide an efficient response to disaster and speedy recovery from it, several important data points are needed, including data from sensors, weather systems, the state of the grid, air-quality data and water-quality data. The scope for data analytics in the field of disaster recovery is huge.

Big Data and rebuilding Christchurch after an earthquake[12]

A geographic information system (GIS) played a key role in the reconstruction of roads and infrastructure in the earthquake-torn city of Christchurch, New Zealand. Rebuilding after the Christchurch earthquake required a great deal of information detailing the spatial position and physical attributes of infrastructure to be collated and disseminated to those planning, designing and constructing repairs and rebuilds. After the September 2010 earthquake, the conceptual architecture of a GIS system was developed, which supported the information and data-management needs of the recovery effort.

The Stronger Christchurch Infrastructure Rebuild Team (SCIRT) GIS viewer was developed to provide a single source of city-wide information in one accessible, current and user-friendly Internet portal. A user was able to see on screen the same information that a series of maps could provide, with interactive layers (nearly 600 of them) showing the location of underground infrastructure, planning

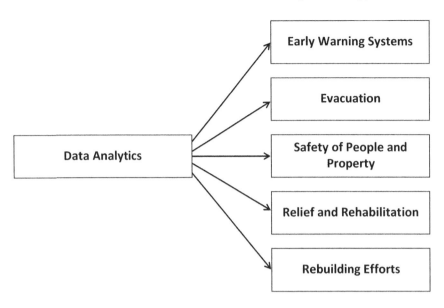

FIGURE 5.5 Data Analytics and Disaster Recovery

zones, archaeological risk areas, project locations and status, cadastral boundaries, title information, picture referencing, pre- and post-earthquake imagery, among an extensive list of information of interest or relevance to the recovery.

Big Data and how the education sector will undergo changes[13]

Big Data in the education sector is likely to bring significant changes from the perspective of students and educational institutions. Big Data is already making an impact on educators, enabling them to reach students in better ways. It will give them a deeper understanding of students' educational experiences and thereby help them evaluate the state of the education system. The overall aim of leveraging Big Data

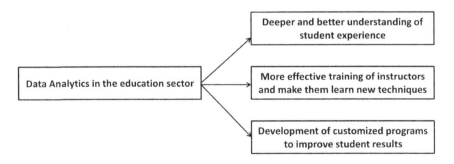

FIGURE 5.6 Data Analytics in the Education Sector

within the educational system is to improve students' results. With Big Data in the education sector, it is possible to monitor student actions, such as how long they take to answer a question or which sources they use for exam preparation, etc.

With the help of Big Data, customized programs for each individual student can be created. As Big Data in the education sector helps improve student results, dropout rates at schools and colleges should also reduce. Educational institutions can use predictive analytics on all the data that is collected to gather insights about future student outcomes. Big Data could also be used to monitor how students are performing in the job market after graduating from college. This would also help future students to choose the right colleges and courses.

Politics, campaigns and elections

Politicians are using Big Data analytics to connect with voters. They are also using social media to target voters in a more structured manner, based on demographics. Mathematics and elections[14] are poles apart. But, anything which is about numbers (and elections of course are about numbers), has a relationship with mathematics. Moreover, with the advent of social media and election analytics,[15] the role of mathematics in elections and how it can influence outcomes is out in the open. It would not be an exaggeration to say that the wave of targeted and data-backed election campaigns which began with Barack Obama's election in 2008[16] is unlikely to be reversed in the near future and, on the contrary, it will likely get stronger and stronger.

2014 general elections in India and data analytics[17]

This trend is not just limited to developed countries. Even in India, the prominent role of election strategists such as Prashant Kishor[18] in the 2012 Gujarat assembly elections (or Vidhan Sabha Elections), followed by the 2014 general elections and then again in the 2015 Bihar elections is proof that election campaigns are getting more and more scientific and less and less intuitive. Similarly, the Indian Prime

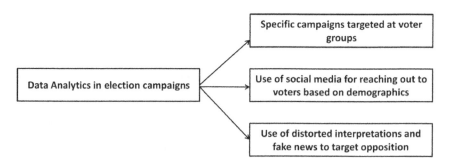

FIGURE 5.7 Data Analytics in Politics and Election Campaigning

Minister, Narendra Modi[19] and Bhartaiya Janata Party[20] (BJP) President, Amit Shah[21] have also accorded special importance to contemporary campaign media and the role of analysis in devising better election campaigns. All other politicians must learn about these aspects quickly; there is simply no other choice for them.

2014 was the first general election in India where social media combined with the use of technology and where advanced data analytics played a crucially important role. The campaign of the BJP and Narendra Modi was not just based on extensive travel by the Prime Ministerial candidate. Mr. Modi addressed as many rallies and meetings as he could, but it was also based on a coordinated and concerted effort by BJP's powerful election-fighting machinery. Both the BJP as a party and Narendra Modi as a leader made a special effort to target the young first-time voters by using these new tools. Other parties were left far behind and, though it is difficult to assess how much this contributed to the end result, it would be impossible to argue that it didn't play an important role.

Election analytics are important because times have changed and technology has become all-pervasive. Election campaigns have also evolved accordingly and the political parties are trying to maximize their impact through key influencing channels. In addition, just like marketing for consumer goods – which has become more targeted and in the way that profiling of customers has become extremely important – elections are also working on similar principles. People do not really want generic communications that don't appeal to them. They only want to listen to messages that are personalized, specific and relevant to them and only then is it possible to strike a chord with them.

The advent of web and social media-based campaigning has increasingly started to play a critical role, at least in urban areas and with the young voters (in the 18 to 25 years age bracket and especially among first-time voters). Because urbanization has been fast in India and the average population is getting younger, election data analytics is an area which cannot be ignored by political parties today. Being responsive and changing with the times creates a positive aura around a party. Voters begin to think that the organization is not rooted in the past and that it can meet the aspirations of a young and modern India.

For example, it is pertinent to highlight that the use of unconventional media for campaigning and fundraising by the Aam Aadmi Party[22] played an important role in its formative years when the party lacked resources to compete with others who were already well-entrenched in the system. Another relevant point is that, in some cases, the margin of victory is really small and even a small swing owing to these factors could mean the difference between a win and a loss. On this score, the BJP is already ahead and the party has been using election analytics and contemporary media for a few years already. The other political parties, at an individual level, need to devise the best possible methods to reach out to the newer categories of voters and to consolidate their existing supporters by remaining relevant to them.

While the role of complex modeling and analytical techniques may not be rare anymore and they do influence the end results, the use of analytics is not limited to these aspects only.

Agriculture: Big Data causing a silent revolution in credit availability

In an article in *Global Trade Review* titled "Big Data drives more finance to African agribusiness,"[23] Shannon Manders has highlighted how the increase in the accumulation of large datasets on agribusiness in Africa is proving helpful to the financing of a sector often overlooked by banks. The article refers to top officials of financing companies emphasizing how the availability of data is making a positive impact on access to financing by bringing about a change in financiers' opinions about financing smaller-scale farming enterprises.

The companies collect and process information to calculate how farmers can achieve profitability and bankability. There is also an "early warning" system in development which helps farmers to discover problems early on and provides them with an overall assessment of their crop. Banks are also becoming more comfortable with weather derivatives and index-based insurance products, which Manders says are becoming more predictable and accurate – purely because of the length of the period of data gathering and due to advancements in technology.

In addition, more specialized financiers, such as leasing companies, are showing an increased interest in investing in the sector. This is primarily because these companies take Big Data a lot more seriously in terms of analyzing affordability. As such, financiers of all kinds across the continent are coming round to the idea of using data when making business-lending decisions. It makes sense because in several African countries, mobile-phone ownership is many times larger than people who are covered by formalized banking systems.

For leasing companies, it is better to use clients' mobile money statements, along with production data, to verify whether they will be able to repay their loans, rather than relying on bank statements. As a result, more and more loans are being made available for clients to start purchasing inputs, such as raw materials, as well as mechanized equipment. The entry of Big Data technology and analytics-based solutions is driving a "change movement" in geographies which were previously untouched by formal banking coverage and were lagging behind because of lack of access to credit.

Finance: can Big Data help in generating above-average returns?[24]

There are already some large institutional investors, such as BlackRock, Schroders and BNY Mellon, who are looking at ways to harness Big Data to improve their investment returns. BlackRock is setting up a new center for research into artificial intelligence. The lab, based in Silicon Valley, is just more proof of how fund managers are aiming to harness technology to improve performance and lower costs. Blackrock comes as no surprise because the firm has always been ahead of its rivals and, being the largest in its field, it is also more willing to experiment. BlackRock already uses insights from various sources, including analyzing traffic through corporate websites, text analysis of earnings, call transcripts and looking at smartphone location data to see where people are shopping.

A 2017 report from Standard and Poor's (S&P) found that 80% of asset managers plan to increase their investments in Big Data over the next 12 months, while only 6% of asset managers argue that Big Data is not important. Also, a report from Barclays found that using alternative data, such as social media feeds, satellite data, or credit card data, is now more prevalent than using economic data, such as employment or inflation figures, or sell-side data, such as analyst reports or broker recommendations. It is clear that asset managers recognize that harnessing this type of data can provide additional insights. But there are concerns as well. For example, will there be any competitive advantage if everybody is looking at the same data?

There may be another problem: does the type of investment required in Big Data mean that larger investment managers gain a strategic advantage? Also, which are the sectors where Big Data will be more useful? For example, there are some sectors where Big Data insights can make a notable difference, such as the financial or consumer sectors. There are other areas where the impact is lesser, such as utilities. In addition, data scientists on their own may not ask the right questions and need to work with an insightful investment team, because knowing what things make a difference matters.

Why the advertising industry is now embracing Big Data[25]

The advertising spends across the various traditional advertising platforms: radio, television and newspapers, are continuously dropping because of technological changes such as Big Data analytics. Traditional advertising once involved circulating ideas and pitches through various departments. Today, working with Big Data companies, advertisers can use these collaborations and partnerships to create original campaigns at a faster pace. Unsurprisingly, new companies that specialize in Big Data analytics have started to gain prominence. It is no shock that marketing and advertising are now embracing Big Data in a big way.

Brands are now in a position to invest in data analytics ecosystems that help them to leverage technological advances to disrupt the traditional advertising ecosystem, which comprised the advertiser, broadcaster/publisher and consumer. Through this, brands are able to effectively mine various consumer datasets and expose them to algorithms that match their brand attributes to effectively curate messaging and placement options that ensure low costs and effective reach. The biggest obstacle is that most companies and brands still lack the expertise necessary to analyze huge amounts of data and make the insights actionable. But they will get there.

Big Data can help make sense of the information gathered, such as retention cost, average transaction value and even customer satisfaction. Big Data can also be used to help create targeted and personalized campaigns that ultimately save money and increase efficiency by targeting the right people with the right products. This is being done by gathering information and learning about user behavior. A consumer's digital footprint today is increasingly valuable in this personalized era of marketing and advertising.

These are the types of insights that can be gained from Big Data. For the marketing and advertising sector this has meant more sophisticated analysis of things such as online activity, point-of-sale transactions and on-the-fly detection of dynamic changes in trends. Big Data will fundamentally alter the ways of doing business and advertising agencies need to change with the shifting environment or they will be left behind. The choice is as simple as that.

In the next chapter

In this chapter, we saw how Big Data and analytics have already started to make an impact on some large enterprises. An increasing number of companies are allocating more time and budget to understand the vast data inside and outside their organizations. The impact on societies is unimaginable as the world is being transformed by Big Data analytics.[26] The key issue is that organizations need to take a flexible approach to Big Data and management must apply considerable thought to what will work for them and they should also be open to the possibility that a quick rethink may be needed at every stage. The need for speed and dynamic decision-making is an absolute necessity for Big Data to succeed and make an impact.

In the next chapter, we will discuss the role of Big Data in creating a sustainable competitive advantage for the user. The ownership of Big Data and the ability to analyze it well gives an edge to organizations over their competitors. The advantage

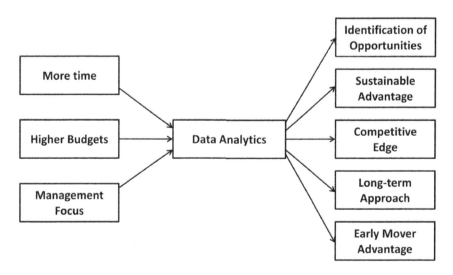

FIGURE 5.8 Big Data and the Organization

of Big Data helps to create opportunities for growth and early movers are likely to reap the maximum benefit. There is also a link between Big Data analytics and innovation. Research has already proved that investment in Big Data is important for the future survival of companies.

Managers should recognize and consider the value of these assets, even if they do not produce short-term performance gains. From a strategic perspective, these findings have important implications because databases are often expensive to produce and maintain. Nevertheless, the use of Big Data on a real-time basis can alert decision-makers to the possible need to quickly change the course of their business and minimize damages when things don't go to plan. This is the theme for the next chapter as we discuss why Big Data matters.

Notes

1 James Freeman Barksdale (Jim Barksdale) is an American executive, formerly President and Chief Investment Officer of the original Equity Investment Corporation, which he founded in 1986. He was the Democratic nominee in the 2016 US Senate election in Georgia. www.biography.com/people/jim-barksdale-9542211 (accessed on 15th April 2019).

2 "Big Data Analytics alters how we study the human genome" by By Jonathan Buckley. www.dataversity.net/big-data-analytics-alters-how-we-study-the-human-genome (accessed on 6th December 2017).

  "Genomics and the role of big data in personalizing the healthcare experience – Increasingly available data spurs organizations to make analysis easier" by Bonnie Feldman. www.oreilly.com/ideas/genomics-and-the-role-of-big-data-in-personalizing-the-healthcare-experience (accessed on 6th December 2017).

  "DNA sequencing and big data open a new frontier in the hunt for new viruses" by Amr Aswad. https://phys.org/news/2017-08-dna-sequencing-big-frontier-viruses.html (accessed on 6th December 2017).

3 "How to identify & acquire new customers using big data" by Vipin Jain. http://customerthink.com/how-to-identify-acquire-new-customers-using-big-data (accessed on 1st December 2017).

4 "Emergence of artificial intelligence and Big Data in healthcare" by Kamal Sachdeva. www.yash.com/blog/ai-bigdata-in-healthcare (accessed on 1st December 2017).

5 "India's Big Data hunt for cures to its mental, ageing-related diseases" by Pankaj Mishra. https://factordaily.com/longform/indias-big-data-huntfor-cures-mental-ageing-related-diseases (accessed on 1st December 2017).

6 "Big Data and rare diseases – Global data exchange makes for faster and more accurate diagnosis" by Johannes Angerer. https://phys.org/wire-news/280659082/big-data-and-rare-diseasesglobal-data-exchange-makes-for-faster.html (accessed on 24th February 2018).

  "Rare diseases and Big Data – Hopes, opportunities and challenges" (no author). www.meduniwien.ac.at/web/ueber-uns/events/detail/event/rare-diseases-and-big-data-hopes-opportunities-and-challenges (accessed on 24th February 2018).

7 "Identifying medical diagnoses and treatable diseases by image-based deep learning" by Daniel S. Kermany, Michael Goldbaum, Wenjia Cai, Carolina C.S. Valentim, Huiying Liang, Sally L. Baxter, Alex McKeown, Ge Yang, Xiaokang Wu, Fangbing Yan, Justin Dong, Made K. Prasadha, Jacqueline Pei, Magdalena Ting, Jie Zhu, Christina Li, Sierra Hewett, Jason Dong. Ian Ziyar, Alexander Shi, Runze Zhang, Lianghong Zheng, Rui Hou, William Shi, Xin Fu, YaouDuan, Viet A.N. Huu, Cindy Wen, Edward D. Zhang, Charlotte L. Zhang, Oulan Li, Xiaobo Wang, Michael A. Singer, Xiaodong Sun, Jie Xu,

Ali Tafreshi, M. Anthony Lewis, Huimin Xia, Kang Zhang. www.cell.com/cell/fulltext/S0092-8674(18)30154-5 (accessed on 24th February 2018).

8 "AI diagnoses eye diseases following Big Data analysis" by Steve Bush. www.electronicsweekly.com/news/research-news/ai-diagnoses-eye-diseases-following-big-data-analysis-2018-02 (accessed on 24th February 2018).

9 "Policy analysis with big data" (speech by Benoît Cœuré, Member of the Executive Board of the ECB). www.ecb.europa.eu/press/key/date/2017/html/ecb.sp171124.en.html (accessed on 1st December 2017).

10 The Abdul Latif Jameel Poverty Action Lab (J-PAL) is a global research center working to reduce poverty by emphasizing that policy is based on scientific evidence and the funding goes to methods which are really effective. www.povertyactionlab.org/about-j-pal (accessed on 1st December 2017).

11 "Cognitive behavioral therapy helped young men in cities in Liberia and United States" *J-PAL Bulletin*, June 2017. www.povertyactionlab.org/sites/default/files/publications/practicing-choices-preventing-crime.pdf (accessed on 1st December 2017).

12 "GIS helps in rebuilding Christchurch after deadly quake strike" by Sinclair Knight Merz. www.geospatialworld.net/article/gis-helps-in-rebuilding-christchurch-after-deadly-quake-strike (accessed on 1st December 2017).

13 "4 ways Big Data is transforming the education sector" by Naveen Joshi. www.allerin.com/blog/4-ways-big-data-is-transforming-the-education-sector (accessed on 1st December 2017).

14 The combinations of these two areas "mathematics and elections" are very nascent. However, since the 2008 US Elections, the area of election analytics has taken on a different dimension. There are studies and media reports that indicate how the BJP was inspired by Barack Obama's victory during the 2008 and 2012 elections in its preparation for the 2014 General elections in India.
   "Big Data, analytics and elections" by George Shen. http://analytics-magazine.org/big-data-analytics-and-elections (accessed on 15th April 2019).
   "Data and elections" (no author). https://privacyinternational.org/topics/data-and-elections (accessed on 15th April 2019).

15 "Lok Sabha Elections 2019: Data and analytics are going to rewrite history" by Richa Bhatia. www.analyticsindiamag.com/lok-sabha-elections-2019-data-and-analytics-are-going-to-rewrite-history (accessed on 15th April 2019); "Vote for analytics! How predictive analytics impacts elections" by AIMS Institutes. https://theaims.ac.in/resources/vote-for-analytics-how-predictive-analytics-impacts-elections.html (accessed on 15th April 2019).

16 Barack Hussein Obama (born 4th August 1961) is an American politician who served as the 44th President of the United States from 2009 to 2017. The first African American to assume the presidency, he was previously the Junior United States Senator for Illinois from 2005 to 2008. He served in the Illinois State Senate from 1997 until 2004. https://barackobama.com (accessed on 15th April 2019).

17 *2019: Will Modi Win?* by Pankaj Sharma and Saurav Sanyal (2018, New Delhi: KW Publishers). www.kwpub.com/BookDetails.aspx?titleId=1380&countryname=India (accessed on 26th February 2018).

18 Prashant Kishor is an Indian political strategist and campaign manager. He is known for his work on the election campaigns for the BJP in the 2014 elections and several other assembly elections. http://indiaconference.com/2019/speakers/prashant-kishor (accessed on 17th April 2019).

19 Shri Narendra Modi is an Indian politician who is the 14th and the current Prime Minister of India. He has been in office since 26th May 2014. Modi is a prominent leader of the Bharatiya Janata Party (BJP) and he was also the Chief Minister of Gujarat from 2001 to 2014. www.narendramodi.in (accessed on 17th April 2019).

20 The Bharatiya Janata Party (BJP) is one of the major political parties in India. In last two general elections, it has been very successful in its electoral track record and has transformed itself into the dominant political force in India. www.bjp.org (accessed on 17th April 2019).

21 Amit Shah is an Indian politician and the President of the BJP. He has been a member of the Gujarat Legislative Assembly a number of times. He is also considered to be a close associate of Prime Minister Shri Narendra Modi. www.amitshah.co.in (accessed on 17th April 2019).

22 Aam Aadmi Party is an Indian political party, formally launched on 26th November 2012 and is currently the ruling party in the state of Delhi. In the 2015 Delhi Legislative Assembly election, the AAP won 67 of the 70 seats in the assembly. www.aamaadmiparty. org (accessed on 2nd December 2017).

23 "Big Data drives more finance to African agribusiness" by Shannon Manders. www. gtreview.com/news/africa/big-data-drives-more-finance-to-african-agribusiness (accessed on 23rd February 2018).

24 "Fund research and insights – Is Big Data the key to bigger investment Returns?" by Cherry Reynard. www.morningstar.co.uk/uk/news/165439/is-big-data-the-key-to-bigger-investment-returns.aspx (accessed on 23rd February 2018).

25 "Why the advertising industry is now embracing big data" by Timothy Oriedo. www. businessdailyafrica.com/analysis/columnists/Why-advertising-industry-is-now-embracing-big-data/4259356-4314512-e1tglfz/index.html (accessed on 24th February 2018); www.businessdailyafrica.com/author-profile/3815404-3840902-view-asAuthor-xuihnj/index.html (accessed on 24th February 2018).

26 "Big Data analytics and sensors: How they are transforming our world" by Rahul Sharma. http://techgenix.com/big-data-analytics (accessed on 1st December 2017).

6

WHY BIG DATA MATTERS

You can use all the quantitative data you can get, but you still have to distrust it and use your own intelligence and judgment.

– Alvin Toffler[1]

Big Data as a competitive advantage: the case of McDonald's[2]

The modern business environment is extremely tough and competitive, even for established companies in their chosen spheres and it is getting tougher. There is relentless pressure from stakeholders to reduce costs, to increase revenues, to become more efficient, and all this while the tightening of regulatory environments and drastic disruptions in traditional business models create huge uncertainty. In a VUCA world (volatile, uncertain, complex and ambiguous), there is always a need to build sustainable competitive advantage and here Big Data can help a lot of companies; for example, the use of Big Data and analytics at McDonald's so that it can provide its customers with a better experience than its competitors without taking a hit on profits.

With annual revenues of $24 billion in 2016, several hundred thousand employees and a presence in almost half the countries in the world, McDonald's is the most powerful QSR (quick-service restaurant) chain in the world. It serves millions of meals every day with amazing efficiency and speed. They generate vast amounts of data, but how do they leverage that data to become more efficient and more competitive? Almost since its very beginnings, McDonald's has been an information-centric organization that makes informed decisions that are reflected in pricing, menu and locations.

The information derived from its predictive analytics is now also used in iterations across design, information and people practices. McDonald's, then, uses analytics to find the trade-offs and changes necessary to find optimal solutions. McDonald's tracks and analyses vast amounts of variables to improve the company and the customer experience. They track in-store traffic, customer interactions, flow across drive-thru restaurants, ordering patterns, point-of-sales data, video data and sensor data. Information derived from this data is used to make iterations in the design of the restaurants, introduce variations to the menus and optimize their training program and supply chain.

The problem in the past was that the data provided by local stores to managers were based on average metrics, which made it difficult to compare the stores and come up with the appropriate actions that needed to take place to improve results. Therefore, McDonald's went from using averages to using trend analytics that provide a lot more insight into what was happening at local stores. They combined datasets and visualized them to better understand the cause and effect in differences between stores. These correlations were used to create more clear, relevant and actionable insights, resulting in savings of money and time across the organization.

One of the examples of such combined metrics is how McDonald's uses Big Data to optimize the drive-thru experience. They analyze and optimize across three different factors: the design of drive-thrus, information that is provided to the customer during the drive-thru and the people waiting in line to order at a drive-thru. There are several variables in these factors and McDonald's will look at them to create an experience which is the most optimal for the customer and at the same time also enhances the profitability for the company.

The net result is better than their competition, of course, keeping variables the same. If used well and analyzed honestly, Big Data and Analytics can be a source of massive competitive advantage for the companies and individuals.

The use of Big Data analytics and innovation – is there a link?

In an interesting paper titled "Big Data – Big Gains? Empirical Evidence on the Link Between Big Data Analytics and Innovation" by Thomas Niebel and others at ZEW (Centre for European Economic Research),[3] researchers have investigated the relationship between the use of Big Data analytics and firms' propensity to innovate, as well as firms' innovation intensity, which is measured by the sales share resulting from new products or services and which constitutes a measure of the market success of the firms' innovations.

The results show that the use of Big Data analytics is associated with a higher propensity to innovate and higher innovation intensity. This is not just true for

FIGURE 6.1   The Link between Big Data and Innovation

modern technologies but applies equally well to mature software systems and data technologies, such as enterprise resource planning software.

As the knowledge production process and innovative output likely differ between manufacturing and service firms, the researchers investigated the potential effects of heterogeneity with regard to these two sectors. Interestingly, the impact is of similar magnitude among firms in the manufacturing and service industries. However, subsequent analyses suggest that firms in the manufacturing and service sectors that apply Big Data rely on different sources of digital information and different data-related firm practices to reap the benefits of Big Data analytics.

Furthermore, while the relation between a firm's use of Big Data and the likelihood of the firm innovating is not contingent on general human capital, it is contingent on firms' investment in IT-specific knowledge and skills. Overall, the results are consistent with the positive returns of Big Data analytics in terms of product innovations. They support the view that knowledge reaped from digitized data by means of Big Data analytics can be a relevant intangible asset in the innovation process.

Adopting new technology – a choice or a compulsion?

In the report, "The Economic Impact of ICT, Centre for Economic Performance, London School of Economics" by Van Reenen, J., Bloom, N., Draca, M., Kretschmer, T. and Sadun, R. (published in 2010),[4] the researchers studied in detail the economic impact of information and communications technology (ICT). The major focus for the research was the post-1995 "productivity miracle" whereby US productivity growth accelerated, led by the contribution of ICT to capital deepening (a consistent increase in capital invested per unit of labor) and a growth in total factor productivity. The economies of the EU did not experience the same type of acceleration.

As a result, while only a 1.8% gap between the levels of US and EU output per worker existed in 1995, this gap grew to 9.8% by 2004. A substantial part of this gap was due to stronger productivity growth in the US's ICT production and market service sectors. This contrast in performance created a major economic puzzle insofar as the European economies experienced the same sharp falls in the prices of ICT producer goods that stimulated ICT investment and productivity in the US. Practically, this implied that there were barriers to economic exploitation of ICT present in Europe.

The report highlighted that ICT capital is characterized by high "above-normal" returns. Evidence from European production functions (the relation

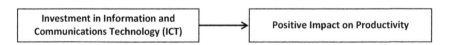

FIGURE 6.2 The Link between ICT and Disproportionate Increase in Productivity

between quantities of physical input and quantities of the output of goods) indicates that a 10% increase in ICT capital is associated with a 0.23% increase in firm productivity, whereas theory suggests that this effect should be closer to 0.16%. In terms of cross-country differences, the firm-level data for Europe indicates that there are clear differences in the impact of ICT between the UK and other European countries.

ICT is found to have a significant role in the process of reallocation. Firms with high levels of ICT are more likely to grow (in terms of employment) and less likely to exit (leave the geographical location). Firms in the top two quintiles of ICT intensity grow around 25–30% faster than other firms and are 4% less likely to exit. Labor and product market regulation are also found to have a role in blunting these forces that determine whether firms survive or fail. That is, low-tech firms in highly regulated economies are more likely to grow and survive than firms in less regulated countries.

The evidence of spillover effects is found in terms of technology adoption. This implies that ICT usage by "neighboring" firms could induce more ICT adoption through learning, network effects or fostering the growth of skilled labor pools. While it is clear that ICT has contributed to innovation (particularly in its role as a "general purpose technology") the nature of this contribution has not been codified. ICT is not strongly associated with increased innovation as measured by formal patents. However, ICT is systematically used by firms within their strategies for product and process innovation.

The report concluded that ICT investment policies should be guided by a different logic to other areas of innovation policy. Rather than being focused on correcting market failures in ICT investment, policies in this area need to focus on assisting the accumulation of a number of complementary factors, principally organizational capital and skills. While subsidies and tax incentives are vital in other areas of innovation policy (such as R&D expenditure) they are not suited to attacking the root causes of Europe's failure to exploit the economic benefits of ICT.

Results may not come tomorrow but you have to invest today

An interesting paper titled "Data Assets and Industry Competition: Evidence from 10-K Filings" by Adam Saunders of the Sauder School of Business, University of British Columbia and Prasanna Tambe of the Stern School of Business, New York University, measured and analyzed the capture, storage, management and analysis of data within US firms from 1996 to 2012.[5] The authors also also analyzed how a shift towards greater use of data in recent years has affected the market value and profitability of firms. The data assets are driving performance dispersion, especially in industries that use IT.

The findings highlight the complementarities and path dependencies of many IT-related intangible assets, such as data assets. The effects of many of these intangible assets – like databases – may not be seen until later periods. It is also the case that investments in activities such as data security and standardization generate more value when put in the context of a firm that made earlier investments in data collection. This observation suggests that managers should recognize and consider the value of these assets, even if they do not produce short-term performance gains.

From a strategic perspective, these findings have important managerial implications because databases are often costly to produce and curate. Therefore, the results suggest that the considerable data assets that have been developed by many firms pose a significant source of competitive advantage, to the extent that they are difficult or time-consuming to replicate.

The findings also have implications for the study of intangible assets and industrial organization. As with previous generations of IT-related technological innovation, current data investments are heavily concentrated within a few sectors where the skills and technologies required for handling massive volumes of data are selected, refined and standardized. However, as with prior technologies, these data-related skills will eventually diffuse across sectors, facilitated by mechanisms such as consulting companies that specialize in Big Data practices or the mobility of new classes of workers (e.g., "data scientists") who can introduce new technologies and practices to firms in other sectors.

Use of personal location data for averting disasters

We are witnessing an explosion in the amount of information available about where people are in the world. Technologies like the Global Positioning System (GPS) allow the quick, precise location of a mobile phone within a few meters and even law-enforcement investigations regularly use such data to establish physical location. From an individual's perspective, the major categories of application for personal location data are linked with smart routing, location-targeted advertising, electronic toll collection, insurance pricing and disaster management. Location data can also be used for urban planning and retail business intelligence.[6]

Can crowds be managed better with personal location data?

On 29th September 2017, in one of the worst disasters of its kind on the Mumbai suburban train network in India, at least 22 people were killed and several others were seriously injured. There was a massive stampede at one of the train stations during the morning rush hour (at Elphinstone Road Railway Station on the Western Suburban line) that led to these deaths and injuries. Elphinstone Road station is a part of the Mumbai suburban network which is operated by Indian Railways, one of the largest train networks in the world.[7]

The incident happened on a foot over-bridge (FOB) linking Elphinstone Road and Parel suburban railway stations in Mumbai during peak hours following sudden rains. There are also unconfirmed rumors that a bridge collapse and a short circuit led to the stampede. According to the initial assessment, the main factor behind this unfortunate incident was the woefully inadequate space and dilapidated infrastructure at Mumbai train stations along with overcrowded suburban trains.

Parel is one of the big commercial hubs in Mumbai and it has turned into a major business center in Mumbai over the years. Hundreds of office complexes have arisen in recent times, attracting huge numbers of people every day. The rush hour sees thousands of people alighting from local trains at Elphinstone Road station and using the FOB to reach the suburban rail network at Parel.

At around 10.40 a.m., when the incident took place, the FOB was heavily crowded. People were standing on the stairs and on the FOB, waiting for the rains to stop. More and more people kept coming to the FOB from train after train. Suddenly a woman standing in the front row slipped on the rain-drenched stairs. Three or four others commuters also slipped, leading to pandemonium at the FOB and then at a major portion of the Elphinstone Road station. Soon after there was a stampede.

This is not the first incident of its kind, as Indian Railways has experienced similar stampedes in the past as well. In February 2013, 37 pilgrims were killed and hundreds were injured in a stampede at a railway station in Uttar Pradesh's Allahabad. In 2010, two persons were killed in a stampede which was triggered by a last-minute change in arrival platforms for two trains at the New Delhi railway station.

Urban planners and crowd management authorities can significantly benefit from the analysis of personal location data. The data can be used to cut congestion and can help in managing large-scale human movement. The use of Big Data on a real-time basis can alert authorities to the risky situations that might arise because of temporary weather factors or an unexpected bottleneck. Had this been in use, it is possible that disasters may not have been averted but the loss of lives and injuries would certainly have been reduced.

In the next chapter

In this chapter we discussed how Big Data can add a significant competitive edge for organizations, although decision makers need to be patient because improvements may not happen as quickly as desired or expected. The question about the importance of Big Data for most people is not "if" or "whether" or "when" anymore, it is only "how" and "why." The choice is about objectives and technologies and not really about whether Big Data can be overlooked.

In the next chapter, we look at some of the important challenges we face when dealing with Big Data. There are challenges in becoming comfortable with the fact that analytics-based decision-making is not inconsistent with instincts-based decision-making. Big Data is only a tool and doesn't replace the need for business leaders. After managers have helped make people comfortable with the need for Big Data analytics in their organizations, the next important questions are: What type of data should be collected? How should it be analyzed? How can it produce actionable insights? And, most importantly, how to measure the return on investment of these technologies?

This discussion leads to another important area, which is whether there is a need to have a regulatory framework or policies for Big Data? Big Data's increasing role raises a number of legal issues which are complex primarily because data is different from other types of asset. Data can be stolen and copied and it is difficult to detect the theft because the same data can be used simultaneously by more than one person. The issues of the ownership of data need to be looked into and there is a burning issue around how to allocate responsibility for the authenticity and genuineness of data.

Notes

1 Alvin Toffler (1928–2016) was an American writer. In 1970, his first major book about the future, *Future Shock*, became a worldwide bestseller and has sold over six million copies. He and his wife Heidi Toffler moved on to examining the reaction to changes in society with another bestselling book, *The Third Wave* in 1980. In it, he foresaw such technological advances as cloning, personal computers, the Internet, cable television and mobile phones. His later focus, via another bestseller, *Powershift* (1990), was on the increasing power of 21st-century military hardware and new technologies. www.britannica.com/biography/Alvin-Toffler (accessed on 15th April 2019).
2 "From Big Data to Big Mac: How McDonald's leverages Big Data" by Dr Mark van Rijmenam. https://datafloq.com/read/from-big-data-to-big-mac-how-mcdonalds-leverages-b/403 (accessed on 6th December 2017).
    "Meet the man helping companies like Wawa and McDonalds make winning decisions using Big Data" by Nick Wells and Eric Chemi. www.cnbc.com/2017/08/16/the-man-helping-wawa-and-mcdonalds-make-winning-decisions-using-big-data.html (accessed on 6th December 2017); https://channels.theinnovationenterprise.com/articles/how-to-use-predictive-data-like-wawa-and-mcdonalds (accessed on 6th December 2017).
    "How to use predictive data like Wawa and Mcdonald's – Two case studies in predictive analytics" by Kayla Matthews. https://businessintelligence.com/bi-insights/from-big-data-to-big-mac-how-mcdonalds-leverages-big-data/(accessed on 6th December 2017).
    "Big McData" (no author). www.predix.com/blog/big-mcdata (accessed on 6th December 2017).
3 "Big Data – Big Gains? Empirical Evidence on the link between Big Data analytics and innovation by Thomas Niebel, Fabienne Rasel and Steffen Viete at the ZEW (Centre for European Economic Research). www.zew.de/en/publikationen/big-data-big-gains-empirical-evidence-on-the-link-between-big-data-analytics-and-innovation/?cHash=6f d3be4c5a5589f1c9323f4b2fa6a88c (accessed on 2nd December 2017).
4 "The economic impact of ICT, Centre for Economic Performance, London School of Economics" by J.Van Reenen, N. Bloom, M. Draca, T. Kretschmer and R. Sadun. http://ec.europa.eu/information_society/newsroom/cf/dae/document.cfm?doc_id=669 (accessed on 2nd December 2017).
5 "Data assets and industry competition: Evidence from 10-K filings" by Adam Saunders. https://papers.ssrn.com/sol3/papers.cfm?abstract_id=2537089 (accessed on 2nd December 2017).
6 In June 2011, McKinsey Global Institute published a report titled "Big Data: The next frontier for innovation, competition, and productivity" by James Manyika, Michael Chui, Brad Brown, Jacques Bughin, Richard Dobbs, Charles Roxburgh and Angela Hung Byers. www.mckinsey.com/business-functions/digital-mckinsey/our-insights/big-data-the-next-frontier-for-innovation (accessed on 29th November 2017).
7 "Mumbai Elphinstone Road stampede highlights: 22 dead, 35 injured; CM announces Rs 5 lakh compensation" by HT correspondents. www.hindustantimes.com/mumbai-news/live-three-dead-30-injured-in-stampede-at-mumbai-s-elphinstone-road-station/story-OjOoREoF9uSwrI4wfm5cDM.html (accessed on 4th December 2017).

"Stampede at Elphinstone Road railway station was waiting to happen" by Manoj Nair. www.hindustantimes.com/mumbai-news/ht-view-a-stampede-at-the-mumbai-station-was-waiting-to-happen/story-QEmsjLoh6WQgxLJOyE0VCI.html (accessed on 4th December 2017).

"Elphinstone Road railway station crush: Major stampedes in past decade" by HT correspondents. www.hindustantimes.com/india-news/commuters-killed-in-crush-at-mumbai-railway-station-major-stampedes-in-past-decade/story-BThI4pyFb1hNeZOv8FrKWM.html (accessed on 4th December 2017)

"Elphinstone Road stampede: How it happened at one of the busiest railway stations in Mumbai" by India Today correspondents. http://indiatoday.intoday.in/story/elphinstone-road-stampede-how-it-happened-mumbai-parel/1/1058382.html (accessed on 4th December 2017).

7

THE CHALLENGES OF BIG DATA

The temptation to form premature theories upon insufficient data is the bane of our profession.

– Sherlock Holmes[1]

Big Data failures are neither rare nor inexpensive: Google Flu Trends

Just like any other tool, Big Data analytics don't guarantee that predictions and inferences will be accurate and lead to insights that are useful and actionable. Another issue is that Big Data is not a substitute for conventional "old-fashioned" data collection, statistical analysis or modeling. There are examples that show that the Big Data ride is bumpy because having lots of data doesn't automatically mean better insights and effective decisions. For example: the Google Flu Trends (GFT).[2] GFT was a web service operated by Google that worked on Big Data analytics to provide estimates of influenza activity. By aggregating and analyzing Google search queries, it attempted to make accurate predictions about flu activity.

This project was launched in 2008 by Google to help predict outbreaks of flu. GFT is now no longer publishing current estimates. The idea behind GFT is that, by monitoring millions of users' health-tracking behaviors online, the large number of Google search queries gathered can be analyzed to reveal if there is the presence of flu-like illness in a population. GFT compared these findings to a historic baseline level of influenza activity for corresponding regions and then reported the activity level as either minimal, low, moderate, high, or intense.

Initially, GFT predictions were largely accurate. However, subsequent reports asserted that GFT predictions were more often inaccurate – especially in the period from 2011 to 2013, when it consistently overestimated flu prevalence. One source of problems was that people making flu-related Google searches may have known very little about how to diagnose flu; searches for flu or flu symptoms may well have been researching disease symptoms that are similar to flu, but are not actually flu. When 80–90% of people visiting the doctor for "flu" don't really have it, you can hardly expect their Internet searches to be a reliable source of information.

The problem was that most people don't know what "flu" is, and relying on Google searches by people who may be utterly ignorant about the illness does not produce useful information. Some of the studies have even claimed that GFT was wrong for 100 out of 108 weeks since August 2011. There was nothing wrong with the GFT algorithm or the data it was looking at, but the searches people were making were not truly representative and this means that the final output was wrong. *And this is not only a problem in the past, there will be enough instances in the future, some known and some not known, which may prove that Big Data doesn't always work.*

Is analysis inconsistent with instincts?

The most critical point is that we shouldn't start with assumptions based on instincts because that will defeat the core purpose of the exercise. An analysis will and should always take precedence over intuitions and instincts. The objective and unbiased analysis can uncover insights that were previously unknown. In addition, since the results from data analysis are always dynamic, as more data gets added and time elapses, the analysis of data is also a continuous and ongoing process.

After the analysis has offered insights and you have prepared a plan of how to act on them, the most difficult part comes next. Knowing what needs to be done and doing it well are two completely different things. You may have the best of plans but it is the execution which counts. It is important to have an execution plan which is win–win and to offer the stakeholders something which adds value to them and is beneficial to you at the same time.

An organization's struggles with data analytics

It is said that the mind can handle about seven pieces of information in its short-term memory. Nobel Prize winner Herbert Simon[3] said,

> In an information-rich world, the wealth of information means a dearth of something else: a scarcity of whatever it is that information consumes. What information consumes is rather obvious: it consumes the attention of its recipients. Hence a wealth of information creates a poverty of attention and a need to allocate that attention efficiently among the overabundance of information sources that might consume it.[4]

These are the challenges that an organization faces with regard to Big Data. In many cases, the real challenge is not the intent but how to move forward with Big Data and how to give data analytics a prominent role. Unfortunately, the truth is that there are no ready-made straightforward answers to some of the questions that any organization struggles with.

- Why do they need to gather data and what type of data should be collected?
- How should it be analyzed and used to produce actionable insights?
- How to measure return on investment from these technologies?

The shortage of talent

A major constraint on realizing complete potential from Big Data is the potential shortage of talent: the set of people with expertise in statistics and computing and the decision makers who know how to understand and use these insights. The demand for deep analytical positions in a Big Data world could exceed the supply. Fresh talent may not be sufficient to fill the gap and it may be necessary to retrain the existing set of employees.

Separating hype from reality

Organizations have to be really careful that they are not investing in Big Data because of hype that surrounds it. As happens with most new technologies, it is difficult for businesses to resist the temptation of over-investing in Big Data,

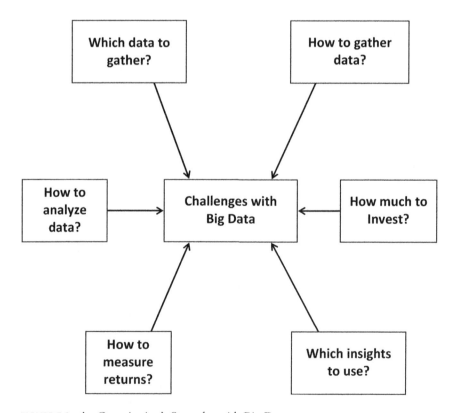

FIGURE 7.1 An Organization's Struggles with Big Data

without truly understanding what can and cannot be achieved. There may be unscrupulous vendors who will promise the Moon but the onus must be on business owners to ensure that they are investing the right amount at the right time and not overdoing it.

The retail industry's struggles

Retail is one of those industries where the pace of data collection is among the highest but this unprecedented access to consumer data poses challenges such as: (a) how to sort and classify data with labels so that it can be used later, (b) how to make the data relevant for customer retention and customer loyalty and to provide them with better experiences, (c) how to enhance profitability without hurting and compromising other processes. Handling the large quanta of data and choosing the right technology are some of the generic issues which every industry faces but there are several challenges specific to the retail industry.[5]

(1) The challenge of recognizing a customer in different channels. How do retailers figure out that the customer who made a purchase at their brick-and-mortar store a week ago and the person who is talking to their call center right now is, in fact, the same person? Any retailer has to deal with millions of customers and this makes it even more complex.
(2) The challenge of optimizing prices without harming financial objectives. Dynamic pricing which is based on real-time inputs is sensible but will only become sustainable from an organization's perspective when prices still align with the pricing strategy and don't ruin sales, margins and profit targets in the process.
(3) The challenge of making sensible and profitable personalized recommendations to customers without annoying them. New customers are especially at risk of being irritated, rather than pleased, by irrelevant product offers, as the recommendation algorithm of the retailer cannot yet know their complete customer histories.

The need for data policies

Big Data's increasing role also raises a number of legal issues which are primarily complex because data is different from other types of assets. Some of the prominent questions and issues around data are:

(1) Data can be stolen and copied. It is difficult to detect theft because the same data can be used simultaneously by more than one person.
(2) Who "owns" data and what is "fair use" of data? Who is responsible for the authenticity and genuineness of the data?
(3) Will there be restrictions on how data can be used and which analyses and uses of technology are acceptable?

(4) Who in the organization should have access to data? Can an organization be forced by the government to share data?

(5) Can an organization purchase data which has been acquired ethically? What happens if the data acquisition was unethical?

In the wake of so much data, it is unarguable that the world needs a stronger cybersecurity and privacy-protection framework. Policymakers need not be intrusive but they can't always leave cybersecurity issues to the wisdom of the market and users. Policymakers need to recognize the potential of using Big Data in an ethical, legal and acceptable manner. There is a need to develop a structure and framework so that data can be used in the most appropriate manner while also creating value.

Since Big Data and analytics is an advancing field and since technological developments happen at a rapid pace, there is also a need for regulators to continuously and consistently involve experts from the private sector. This is relevant because one very important challenge for regulators is to draft and implement regulation in such a way that it doesn't become intrusive and is not a hindrance in regular operations. If the regulation is leading to inefficiencies and more bureaucratic procedures in an organization, then fundamentals are being compromised. Sooner or later, it will start to hurt.

Cost is another dimension. If the cost of compliance, both in terms of time and monetary implications, becomes prohibitive it will defeat the basic purpose of regulation. For this to happen effectively and successfully, the regulator needs to come down from their ivory towers and be aware of realities on the ground. They also need to be given enough enablers by the government in terms of resources and freedom. Regulators need to understand and draw a line when deciding the areas where market wisdom works best and where regulation in the form of a nudge, incentive or penalty is needed.

The first step for regulators is to create more awareness about data protection, cyber security and respect for privacy issues. The regulator has to be sympathetic that companies and technology leaders need to be aware of the impact of the adoption of these technologies and their advancements. They may not always have the capability and the bandwidth with to think about the policy implications of these issues clearly and come up with correct conclusions. This can be better achieved by raising their sensitivity about these implications and by knowing how to better address these challenges.

Big Data and associated technologies are in an evolving phase and there is still a lot to discover, even for technologists. Hence, it is very possible that government and regulator will keep trying to play catch-up with advances in technology and they may remain a step behind. But that is not the key point nor should it be a reason for them to get disheartened about the task in hand. The purpose of any regulation, for that matter, is much larger. It is to provide a level playing field for technologies and companies, make the user more responsible and aware of his or her actions and, if possible, to try to reduce and eliminate inefficiencies and inconsistencies.

In the next chapter

In this chapter, we discussed how organizations have to be careful that they are not investing in Big Data because of any associated hype. Big Data's increasing role also raises a number of legal issues because data is different from other assets. In the wake of so much data, the world needs a stronger cybersecurity and privacy-protection framework. Policymakers need not be intrusive but they can't always leave cybersecurity issues to the wisdom of markets and users alone. Policymakers need to recognize the potential of using Big Data in an ethical, legal and accept-able manner.

In the next chapter, we take a look at the policy issues which are becoming relevant because of the exponential growth of Big Data. As Big Data become more important, the policy issues linked to privacy and data security will continue to become more and more crucial. Collecting the data is the easier part but the bigger challenge lies with the protection of privacy and the security of sensitive informa-tion. It is easy to see that, as more data is stored, the more vital it is to ensure its security. This requires a coordinated response and companies have to face these issues on a regular basis.

The other important issue that we discuss in the next chapter is how data ownership should be valued in the case of companies. When Big Data offers a competitive advantage and may be the difference between victory and defeat in the market place, why should financial statements not reflect this? Why the invest-ments made in data accumulation by companies or the losses borne by e-commerce companies to get data rich quickly should not be treated as an investment in creat-ing business assets.

Notes

1 Sherlock Holmes is a fictional private detective created by British author Sir Arthur Conan Doyle. First appearing in print in 1887 (in "A Study in Scarlet"), the charac-ter's popularity became widespread with the first series of short stories in *The Strand Magazine*, beginning with "A Scandal in Bohemia" in 1891. Additional tales appeared from then until 1927, totalling four novels and 56 short stories. www.arthurconandoyle. com/sherlockholmes.html (accessed on 15th April 2019); www.britannica.com/topic/ Sherlock-Holmes (accessed on 15th April 2019).
2 "What we can learn from the epic failure of Google flu trends" by David Lazer and Ryan Kennedy. www.wired.com/2015/10/can-learn-epic-failure-google-flu-trends (accessed on 6th December 2017).
   "Why Google flu is a failure" by Steven Salzberg. www.forbes.com/sites/stevensalzberg/ 2014/03/23/why-google-flu-is-a-failure/#5ea2eb665535 (accessed on 6th December 2017).
   "New flu tracker uses Google search data better than Google" by Beth Mole. https:// arstechnica.com/science/2015/11/new-flu-tracker-uses-google-search-data-better-than-google (accessed on 6th December 2017).
   "The parable of Google flu: Traps in Big Data analysis" by David Lazer, Ryan Kennedy, Gary King and Alessandro Vespignani. http://science.sciencemag.org/content/343/6176/ 1203 (accessed on 6th December 2017).
3 Herbert Simon (1916–2001) was an American political scientist whose research ranged across the fields of cognitive psychology, computer science, public administration, eco-nomics, management, philosophy of science and sociology. He was a professor at Carnegie

Mellon University. With almost a thousand very highly cited publications, he is one of the most influential social scientists of the 20th century. www.nobelprize.org/prizes/economic-sciences/1978/simon/biographical (accessed on 15th April 2019).

4 Herbert Simon is known for the theory of bounded rationality, a theory about economic decision-making. Contrary to the tenets of classical economics, Simon maintained that individuals do not seek to maximize their benefit from a particular course of action since they cannot assimilate and digest all the information. https://excellentjourney. net/2015/04/28/a-poverty-of-attention (accessed on 9th December 2017); www.economist.com/node/13350892 (accessed on 9th December 2017).

5 "How retailers can tackle 3 Big Data challenges" by Alexander Bekker. www.cmswire.com/digital-experience/how-retailers-can-tackle-3-big-data-challenges (accessed on 23rd February 2018).

8

BIG DATA

The key questions

> Whether it's Facebook or Google or the other companies, that basic principle that
> users should be able to see and control information about them that they themselves
> have revealed to the companies is not baked into how the companies work. But it's
> bigger than privacy. Privacy is about what you're willing to reveal about yourself.
> – *Eli Pariser*[1]

Data is valuable for everyone, including criminals: the Uber incident

Uber paid hackers $100,000 for silence about a cyberattack that exposed 57 million people's data.[2] In November 2017, the popular ride-hailing app Uber disclosed that its executives concealed an October 2016 cyber attack. This included a payment of $100,000 to the two hackers who had accessed the data in exchange for their promise to keep quiet and delete the information. Uber acknowledged that two individuals in October 2016 had accessed and downloaded data on 57 million Uber riders and drivers that was stored in a third-party infrastructure system.

As part of the cyberattack, the names and driver's license numbers of around 600,000 drivers were accessed. Fifty-seven million Uber users also had their information exposed, including names, emails, and mobile phone numbers, the company said. Uber's then-CEO Travis Kalanick first learned of the incident in November 2016 when Uber was finalizing a settlement with the Federal Trade Commission for privacy violations. The company instead chose to pay the hackers $100,000 to delete the information and stay quiet about the incident.

The leak of names, phone numbers, and email addresses represents valuable data for hackers with criminal intent because with the help of this information they can combine it with other data leaks to carry out identity theft. The more sensitive driver data that was leaked might offer even more useful private information for fraudsters to exploit. This reflects another larger problem that, as a user, once you share your personal information with someone there is no control of how that information will be used, stored or disseminated.

Another issue is that Uber knew about it and for more than twelve months it failed to disclose the breach. There is no reason to be assured that this will not happen again or that this is unique to Uber. *The first response may be "hide" and "push under the carpet" for many of the sites and databases where we share our information, and that is not a pleasant thought.*

The big players and are they blocking access to the playground?

The first and one of the most important challenges which societies face concerns what kind of transformations their economic engines might undergo because of Big Data. The important difference between Big Data and several other industries we looked at earlier is that the dominance of a particular company or group of companies might throttle competition forever. Whether we call it "first-mover advantage" or attribute it to the "strength of the incumbent" or simply accept it as the inherent characteristic of this industry, it is an undeniable fact that, beyond a point, the dominance of leading players leads to a situation that doesn't allow many new companies to join the game and compete.

The idea is not to find a scapegoat or penalize companies which are big and strong because of their relentless focus on efficiency and excellence, but to at least be aware of the complete range of consequences. There is a need to be sensitive about these issues and take proactive measures so that we can create an environment which is not stifling for new joiners, without compromising too much on users' interests and efficiency in the system. There may be no easy answers but we need to seriously consider if a rethink is required on what we mean by "monopoly" and what we should classify as restrictive business practices.

Big Data industries – winner takes all[3]

How many auto companies can you name? Of course there are many, including Toyota, General Motors, Daimler, Hyundai, Honda, Nissan, Ford, Suzuki, Volkswagen and BMW.

How many consumer companies can you name? Again, there are many of these including Unilever, Procter & Gamble, Reckitt Benckiser, Nestlé, Johnson & Johnson, Coca Cola, Pepsi, Philip Morris and Mondelez.

How many pharmaceutical companies can you name? Once again, there are many of these and they include Pfizer, Astra Zeneca, Glaxo SmithKline, Sanofi, Merck, Bayer and Roche.

Now, let us see look at some other industries.

How many competitors of Google can you name? On the one hand there seems to be many, including eBay, Yahoo, AOL, Expedia, and Facebook. Looked at in another way, there are none. Even Eric Schmidt has said that Amazon or Apple are the closest competitors for Google. If we only look at search engine businesses, Baidu from China is the closest competitor but that is more because the Chinese government makes it difficult for companies in the information-dissemination business to operate in China. However, no other company has the scale of Google.

How many competitors of Facebook can you name? These would be Instagram, Snapchat and LinkedIn. There is also WeChat in China and Vkontakte in Russia. But again, none of these have the scale of Facebook.

- How many competitors of WhatsApp can you name?
- How many competitors of Amazon can you name?
- How many competitors of Alibaba can you name?
- How many competitors of Microsoft can you name?
- How many competitors of LinkedIn can you name?
- How many competitors of Instagram can you name?
- How many competitors of YouTube can you name?

Two things are very clear: the "new economy" companies do not need a large workforce and these new businesses are not conducive to competition. The case of Big Data is not very different. Just like other Internet-based businesses, Big Data, at least in terms of its applications and technology, is a "winner takes all" industry to a large extent. There is very little space for smaller competitors. Small and large competitors cannot survive in "peaceful coexistence." In the Big Data business, a company which is 2x larger than its nearest competitor (not necessarily because it is better or has better products or services) will grow 3x or 4x larger in a short space of time. Sooner or later, the larger competitor will elbow out the smaller competitor.

We can have many large fast-moving consumer goods (FMCG) or auto or pharmaceutical companies but it is doubtful if we can have many large Amazons or Facebooks. There can be many successful multinational companies in the "old-economy industries." And similarly, at a local level, every country can have many local FMCG, automobile and pharmaceutical companies which are influential and can do good business. So, these industries from the old economy are decentralized. However, only a handful of elite companies would get to keep majority gains in Big Data-based industries and power will be concentrated in the hands of just a few corporations.

The data security challenge

As Big Data becomes more important, the policy issues linked to privacy and data security also become more important. Collecting the data is a relatively easy part of the process but the bigger challenge is the protection of privacy and security of sensitive information. It is easy to see that as more data is stored, the more vital it is to ensure its security. Hackers' attacks on IT systems are becoming more lethal and new viruses and security breaches are becoming more powerful. This requires a coordinated response and companies have to face these issues on a daily basis.

Breaches of data security can lead to great financial losses and reputational damage for a company. How to protect sensitive data is of the utmost importance, as incidents related to data leaks have demonstrated. It is no surprise that many citizens and organizations around the world regard this collection of massive amounts of data and information with deep suspicion and skepticism because they think it is a serious intrusion of their privacy. Personal data, being the most sensitive, is always at risk of being leaked.

UIDAI (Aadhaar) and the privacy debate

The Unique Identification Authority of India (UIDAI) is a statutory authority established under the provisions of the Aadhaar (Targeted Delivery of Financial and Other Subsidies, Benefits and Services) Act, 2016 ("Aadhaar Act 2016") on 12th July 2016. It was established by the Government of India, under the Ministry of Electronics and Information Technology. Prior to its creation as a statutory authority, UIDAI was functioning as an attached office of the then Planning Commission (now NITI Aayog). Later, on 12th September 2015, the government revised the Allocation of Business Rules to attach the UIDAI to the Department of Electronics & Information Technology of the then Ministry of Communications and Information Technology.[4]

UIDAI was created with the objective to issue unique identification numbers (UID), named as "Aadhaar," to all residents of India, and that were: (a) robust enough to eliminate duplicate and fake identities, and (b) able to be verified and authenticated in an easy, cost-effective way. The first UID number was issued on 29th September 2010. UIDAI is responsible for Aadhaar enrolment and authentication, including the operation and management of all stages of the Aadhaar life-cycle; developing the policy, procedure and system for issuing Aadhaar numbers to individuals; performing authentication; and it is also required to ensure the security of personal-identity information and authentication records of individuals.

Aadhaar, which means "foundation" is a 12-digit unique-identity number issued to all Indian residents, based on their biometric and demographic data. The data is collected by the UIDAI and Aadhaar is currently the world's largest biometric ID system, with over 1.171 billion enrolled members as of 15th August 2017. Over 99% of Indians aged 18 and above are enrolled in Aadhaar. However, owing to increasing concerns around privacy, the potential for surveillance, and the exclusion of eligible beneficiaries from welfare schemes through the leveraging of Aadhaar-based systems, the validity of the Aadhaar project is being challenged in the Supreme Court of India.

On 23rd September 2013, the Supreme Court of India issued an interim order saying that "no person should suffer for not getting Aadhaar" as the government cannot deny a service to a resident if s/he does not possess Aadhaar, as it is voluntary and not mandatory. In another interim order on 11th August 2015, the

Supreme Court of India ruled that "UIDAI/Aadhaar will not be used for any other purposes except PDS, kerosene and LPG distribution system" (which order was later amended to include the Mahatma Gandhi National Rural Employment Guarantee Scheme, all types of pensions schemes, the Employee Provident Fund and the Prime Minister Jan Dhan Yojana), and made it clear that, to be able to access these facilities, an Aadhaar card is not mandatory.

On 27th March 2017, the Supreme Court affirmed that Aadhaar is not mandatory for accessing benefits under welfare schemes, although it can be mandatory for other purposes (such as income-tax filing, bank accounts, etc.). On 9th June 2017, the Supreme Court of India partially blocked a legal provision (Section 139AA of the Income Tax Act) which mandated an individual to link their Aadhaar for filing their income-tax returns. However, reports of exclusion from welfare benefits due to technological breakdown of the Aadhaar system, from various states, have continued to appear.

On 24th August 2017, the Supreme Court of India delivered a landmark verdict on the right to privacy. The court declared the right to privacy as a fundamental right intrinsic to the right to life. The order affects all 1.34 billion Indians. The apex court overruled previous judgments on the privacy issue and said that:

> privacy is not lost or surrendered merely because the individual is in a public place. Privacy attaches to the person since it is an essential facet of the dignity of the human being . . . . The right of privacy is a fundamental right. It is a right which protects the inner sphere of the individual from interference from both State, and non-State actors and allows the individuals to make autonomous life choices . . . .

Some civil liberty groups, like the Citizens Forum for Civil Liberties and the Indian Social Action Forum (INSAF), have opposed the project over privacy concerns.

As of November 2017, a five-judge constitutional bench of the Supreme Court is yet to hear various associated cases relating to the validity of Aadhaar on various grounds, including privacy, surveillance and exclusion from welfare benefits. Despite Aadhaar's validity being challenged in the court, the central government has pushed citizens to link their Aadhaar numbers with a host of services including mobile SIM cards, bank accounts, the Employee Provident Fund, etc. and a large number of welfare schemes including, but not limited to, the Mahatma Gandhi National Rural Employment Guarantee Act, the Public Distribution System and old-age pensions. Recent reports suggest that HIV patients have been forced to discontinue treatment for fear of identity breach because access to treatment has become contingent on producing their Aadhaar.

There are several issues with Aadhaar, including: (a) feasibility concerns – implementation without any cost–benefit or feasibility study, (b) lack of legislation and privacy concerns, (c) the legality of sharing data with law enforcement, (d) security concerns and (e) fraud, because obtaining an Aadhaar card does not require significant documentation, with multiple options available. In theory, the use of biometric facilities should reduce or eliminate duplication. So it may be possible to obtain the card under a false name and there have been cases where the biometrics requirements have been circumvented and potentially fraudulent Aadhaars have been issued.

However, the biggest issue of all concerns data security and privacy. The amount of detailed personal information being collected is extremely important to the individual. However, once collected, it is not being treated with the required sensitivity to the concerns of privacy. Major financial transactions are linked with information connected to the Aadhaar. A data leak is a great opportunity for hackers and criminals. A big question is whether the government department concerned and various other agencies that collect this information, including banks, etc., can be trusted to maintain the secrecy of all this sensitive information.

Another case concerns Aadhaar data collected by Reliance Jio, which was leaked online and may now be widely available to hackers. UIDAI confirms that more than 200 government websites were publicly displaying confidential Aadhaar data – although it has been officially removed now, leaked data leaked be scrubbed from hackers' databases. On 12th July 2017 the Aadhaar Card privacy issue was discussed at the Supreme Court of India. A report from the Center for Internet and Society suggests about 135 million Indians' records may have been leaked.

Wikileaks tweeted on 25th August 2017 that the same American supplier of fingerprint and Iris scanning equipment that collaborated with the CIA to identify Osama Bin Laden was also supplying equipment to India. The complex structure of ownerships is detailed in an article at www.fountainink.in. Concerns were raised way back in 2011 in the *The Sunday Guardian* regarding due process not being followed and contracts being hand over to entities with links to the FBI with a past history of leaking data across countries. How the CIA can hack and access the Aadhaar database using the secret Expresslane project is documented in a report on the GGI News website and saved in an archive lest it be forcefully removed. Further communications have also identified the clauses under which data may have freely flowed to foreign agencies due to the nature and wording of Aadhaar contracts.

Is data an asset and should we tax companies for its ownership?

When data is seen as *the new oil* and has become an important competitive advantage for organizations, it is imperative that we should look at data as an asset. There are many reasons to support this thought and why data should be seen as a tangible asset:

- Data creation, accumulation, storage and maintenance involve costs and require significant investment. Once these investments are made, data can be used to earn revenues and build customer tractions. So, there is a profit motive behind the accumulation and analysis of data. Hence, it is no different to any other tangible or intangible asset.

- Data ownership and capability could be a differentiator between two otherwise similar companies and investors tend to believe that data has a value as reflected by market evaluations. The number of companies with data as their strength is increasing in the list of the most valuable global companies. The acquisition of several loss-making start-ups at exorbitant valuations in the past confirms this hypothesis.

The concept of depreciation

In simple terms, depreciation is an accounting tool by which a company can allocate the cost of a tangible asset over its useful life. In the case of intangible assets, a similar concept called amortization is used. Loosely speaking, amortization refers to the allocation of a one-time payment for intangible assets over the asset's useful life or the duration which is permissible under accounting standards. But, in order to understand why this concept is needed, a little bit of perspective on what constitutes the cost of doing business may help.

Let us say you are running a café. A customer walks in and she orders a cappuccino and some cookies. It is easy for you to calculate the directly attributable cost for this order in the costs of milk, sugar, flour and other ingredients in the cookies. These are strictly variable costs and you don't incur them if the customer does not place her order. There are a few other variable operational costs which may not be directly attributable to a particular customer or an individual but you can still see them. For example, the electricity bill which you incur as you run your coffee machine, oven and air conditioner, or the salary of your assistant, or the rent for the premises. Some of these may be called overheads but all of these costs need to be paid either in cash or, if you are lucky, through credit.

However, there are some other costs which are a little more difficult to understand. For example, your coffee machine may undergo wear and tear and there is also a risk that it may become obsolete and you may be required to replace it after a few years. The fittings and fixtures may need to be changed over time. The van you use for bulk deliveries and the billing machine or computer you use will also be valued much less after a while. If you own the premises, although you may be saving on rent, you may be required to incur regular maintenance expenses. The fact that many of these fixed items will require, over time, repairs, replacement or upgrade, means that you need to save money for these expenses or investments.

Methods of depreciation and salvage value

As per law, businesses depreciate the value of long-term assets over a finite period of time for tax and accounting purposes. The depreciation expense does not represent a cash transaction, but it indicates how much of an asset's value has been used up over time. For example, if a company buys a piece of equipment for $10,000, which the company expects to use for ten years, it can either write the entire cost of the asset off in year one, or it can write the value of the asset off over the life of the asset, i.e. ten years.[5]

This means the company, in its account statements, does not have to write off the entire $10,000, even though it paid out that amount in cash. Instead, the company only has to expense the proportionate amount, which is equivalent to the expense in one year. How much that amount to depends on the method being used to calculate the depreciation. For example: two of the more common methods are: straight-line vs. double-declining methods.

To understand these, we also need to know the concept of salvage value. Salvage value is the estimated value that the owner receives when the item is sold at the end of its useful life. The salvage value is used in conjunction with the purchase price to determine the amount of annual depreciation of the asset. In the straight-line depreciation method, an equal amount of depreciation is recognized each year. In an accelerated method of depreciation (such as double-declining), the company recognizes more depreciation in the early years and less in the later years of the asset's useful life.

Assume, for example, that a company buys a machine at a cost of $5,000 and that the machine has a salvage value of $1,000 and a useful life of five years. Based on these assumptions, the annual depreciation using the straight-line method is: ($5,000 cost minus $1,000 salvage value) over five years, or $800 per year. The asset's depreciable base is the cost less salvage value, or $4,000, which is apportioned over five years.

Ignoring "non-cash" expenses overestimates profitability of business

For this reason, when you look at the assets and liabilities of a business, the permanent fixtures will continue to decline in their value over time unless new fixed assets are being added. This "fictitious" or "intangible" expense from a cash inflow and cash outgo perspective provides for the replacement of these assets in future. In addition, the profit and loss statement also needs to capture this expense. This is important to reflect the true profitability of the business. If we are only looking at the cash expenses and not considering the decline in the value of fixed assets, which are essential for business, we are underestimating real expenses and overestimating the profitability of the business we are evaluating.

There are several businesses where the investment needed in fixed assets is many times more than the regular, operating expenses. For example, if you own an airport or a freeway, your operating expense will be minuscule and, on the basis or regular income and day-to-day expenses, you would seem to be hugely profitable. But the amount of money you invested to build this airport or the freeway would have been huge and this doesn't get captured in the regular operating expenses. This asset will not last forever and obviously has a finite life. The fixed-asset investment also needs to be recovered by the company that built it over the course of its "useful life". Essentially, this is the concept that depreciation as an expense is a non-cash item and is different from other expense items that involve cash outgoings in the financial year, for which an income statement is prepared. However, it is important not to ignore them if a true picture of business profitability, estimated expenses and profits is to be achieved.

Non-cash items and items with a timing mismatch

Depreciation is not the only such non-cash item. Accounting standards need to carefully consider all the possible items which are non-cash in nature and/or which have a timing mismatch, to efficiently capture the health of a business. There are some other simple examples and they can exist on both sides: expenses and income.

(1) If you are a database company and you charge your customers a one-time subscription fee for five years' membership, the income has to be accounted equally across all five years and not just in the year when the customer bought the subscription.

(2) If you are supplying a product or service every year for which you receive the payment only after three years, the income has to be apportioned and accounted for every year instead of being included in the last year when it is actually received.

(3) If you enter into a barter trade with another entity, despite it being a non-cash item, those expenses and liabilities, or income and assets, need to be reflected in your financial statements.

What if you don't consider these intricacies? What happens when you do not consider all non-cash items or items with a timing mismatch in your financial statements? Well, sometimes these mistakes can be honest and genuine but sometimes they are malicious deliberately criminal. By using loopholes in accounting standards, businesses can actually advance their earnings and postpone their expenses and make themselves look significantly more profitable than they are in reality. This usually does not happen without the auditors being complicit in the fraud. The repercussions are widespread and far-reaching. However, at the base level, every story of accounting fraud is a story of greed, deceit and the need for bigger lies to hide smaller lies.

The Enron saga[6]

One of the most infamous examples of accounting fraud is the Enron scandal. The scandal, which is about 15 years old, eventually led to the bankruptcy of the Enron Corporation – a large US-based multinational energy company – and the dissolution of Arthur Andersen, which was one of the five largest audit and accountancy partnerships in the world at that point. Enron was the largest bankruptcy in American history at that time and it was also one of the biggest audit failures.

Enron was formed in 1985 by Kenneth Lay after merging Houston Natural Gas and InterNorth. The company – by exploiting accounting loopholes, special-purpose entities, off-balance items, a large number of subsidiaries and related part transactions plus poor financial reporting – was able to hide billions of dollars of debt from failed deals and projects. The chief financial officer of Enron and other senior executives not only misled Enron's board of directors and the audit committee about high-risk accounting practices, but also pressured Arthur Andersen to ignore the issues.

But, as tends to happen with such cases, they could only hide for so long. When the financial misreporting and the negligence of auditors finally came to light, it was a major wake-up call for the whole world.

Data is the new oil

In one of its editions in May 2017, *The Economist* wrote that the world's most valuable resource is no longer oil, but data.[7] The article was commenting on how the new data economy demands a new approach to antitrust rules. The article says that data today has the same importance that oil had a century ago. Data is the "oil" of the digital era. The main companies that own this new resource: Alphabet (Google's parent company), Amazon, Apple, Facebook and Microsoft, are the five most valuable listed firms in the world. Their profits are surging. Amazon captures half of all dollars spent online in America. Google and Facebook accounted for almost all the revenue growth in digital advertising in the US last year. Such dominance has prompted calls for the tech giants to be broken up, as Standard Oil was in the early 20th century.

The article goes on to say that access to data provides the core competitive edge of these companies. The tech giants' surveillance systems span the entire economy: Google can see what people search for, Facebook what they share, Amazon what they buy. These companies can see when a new product or service gains traction, allowing them to copy it or simply buy the upstart before it becomes too great a threat. Many think Facebook's $22bn purchase in 2014 of WhatsApp, a messaging app with fewer than 60 employees, falls into this category of "shoot-out acquisitions" that eliminate potential rivals. By providing barriers to entry and early-warning systems, data can stifle competition.

How about data as an asset on the balance sheet?

What is the most important asset of Coke, the corporation? Is it the bottling plants? Is it the distribution network? Is it Coke's presence in almost every country in the world? What is the most important asset of McDonald's, the corporation? Is it the food joints? Is it the millions of dollar of sales every day? Is it McDonald's ubiquitous presence? All of these things are important but they are not the core of Coke or McDonald's. It is the brand. Despite various estimates on the brand value of Coke or McDonald's, it is difficult to quantify with precision how much the brand is worth. Almost everyone would agree that brand has value but there is rarely consensus on its precise value. This is because it is "intangible." You can't simply count it.

Why is Facebook free? Why does Google provide so much storage space for customers without charging them anything? Why does Amazon burn billions of dollars in markets like India? Why will Uber continue to make losses in an attempt to gain more and more users? It is because these companies are receiving something intangible from their users. Their users are sharing details about themselves with these companies and this is a huge amount of information being generated every second. Users are telling Facebook about their likes and dislikes, their political preferences, their hobbies and interests. They are telling Google what they are searching for. They are telling Amazon what they buy and how often. They are telling Uber where they travel to.

So, what is the most important asset of tech companies? It is, simply, data and nothing else. A competitor with deep pockets can replicate the entire physical infrastructure these companies have but cannot replicate the data these companies have. By burning more cash, some other corporation may even attract more users than these companies. But nothing will give that competitor access to the data which has already been accumulated. This data provides immense firepower to these companies to offer tailor-made services to their users either directly or indirectly and that is the edge they have. Data may be intangible but it has value.

The relevance of depreciation for data

What about depreciation in reverse? What about an asset that is getting more valuable each passing second, each passing day and each passing week? We have discussed two things so far: (a) tangible assets depreciate in value with time and this means a non-cash expense, (b) data has value and is an intangible asset. Interestingly, this asset is increasing in size continuously and consistently. What does this mean and how does this asset get created? This asset is being created by artificially lowering the income (charging less to customers, like Uber, or charging nothing, like Google) or inflating the expense (offering a competitive price which is at times less than the purchase price, as Amazon does in several cases) or sometimes even doing both.

It is not illegal and not against standard accounting standards but practically speaking the "data bank" is being created by misreporting the income statement by showing lower incomes and/or higher expenses and, as a result, a much-reduced profitability. This misreporting is different from conventional misreporting where management does so with the criminal intention of hiding a company's true financial position to either fool investors or to inflate incentives linked to financial performance. This is a slightly different case whereby tech companies forego a significant part of their present-day earnings to capture and build data. When an organization is creating an asset for the future by reducing its current profitability, the authorities and accounting standards should address this anomaly.

One way to do this is for tax authorities to have norms on how this asset called "data" needs to be valued and organizations should be taxed appropriately and not on the basis of what they earn today and report in their profit and loss statements. The taxation should be based on real and not notional earnings and intangible, non-cash items such as data should be included in the purview of taxation. Ideally, the tech giants and leading e-commerce companies should not be allowed to get away with paying lower taxes just because they are reporting smaller profits or because they are incurring apparent losses. They are collecting and accumulating data and they should pay tax on this asset and the income associated with it.

The FANGs and others should be taxed for the data they own

The financial muscle of companies Facebook, Amazon, Netflix and Google (collectively known as FANGs) puts them at the forefront of development on data and its use for increasing profitability. But they are not alone. Companies like Microsoft and several others are also working in this direction and investing huge sums of money in the development of data and related capabilities. It can be argued that it is not always necessary for massive resources to lead to a sustainable competitive advantage. But hardly anyone would deny that investment matters. The kind of advancements that companies with strong war chests can hope to achieve with Big Data by throwing money at the issue will be significantly more than companies that don't have that kind of money to invest.

These tech giants can be taxed on the value of the data they own. Considering there are so many experts and independent agencies trying to figure out the quantifiable value of intangible assets such as "brand" or "reputation," it should not be too difficult to value the "data" asset. The estimates would require that expected benefits accruing to the company which owns this data are quantified and this non-cash, intangible asset be put on the balance sheet and any increase or decline captured in income statements.

It is possible that taxing these companies will not deter them from investing in Big Data. However, the objective is not to stop the flow of investment into Big Data. There is no amount of tampering and creation of artificial barriers that can stop the market forces because they are just too powerful. If companies see value in making these investments in Big Data, they will continue to make them irrespective of tax or not. However, the most important idea here is to create a level playing field so that unjustified tax-saving avenues are not available to companies regardless of their interest and work in the area of Big Data.

Should tech companies be allowed to benefit from user data?

Let us also look at the issue of ownership of this data. Collectively, the user data which belongs to individual users become very powerful when the number of users is very high and when data collection is more frequent and covers a wider range. This is because of "network effect"[8] which is the name for the impact that one user of a good or a service has on the value of that product to others. When a network effect is present, the value of a product or service is dependent on the number of other people using it.

The classic example is the telephone, where a greater number of users increases the value to each. Online social networks work similarly, with sites like Twitter and Facebook increasing in value for each member as more users join. Over time, positive network effects can create a bandwagon effect as the network becomes more valuable and more people join, creating a positive feedback loop.

Nevertheless, the data still belongs to the user and why should companies be allowed to financially benefit from the use of this data? The free or subsidized service offered by a tech or e-commerce company is in reality a trap. Once the user is hooked, the data which is being collected on them will be used by these companies to either sell the user services and products by the company or the advertisers on the platform.

You can argue that conventional advertising is similar. Companies sell you products and services and from that income they allocate money to their publicity budgets and advertising. However, the difference lies in the fact that you are paying for these services and products because you want to use them – because of brand pull or quality of the products that aew owned by these companies — while, in the case of tech, it is your data which is being used by the companies to make commercial gains.

Should the tech giants pay users for using their services?

Another way to look at how to resolve the conflict over who should get to keep the gains is how these tech giants have created value for themselves. The value of a tech company is directly linked to factors such as: how many people are on the platform, how often they use it and the data trail they leave behind. The end users of the platform are the ones who contribute the most towards the sky-high valuations of these companies so why should they not gain when the value of a company increases? They also need to be rewarded for the success of a platform and should be able to participate in its wealth creation.

This implies not only that the services of a company like Facebook or Google should be free, the users should also be paid for enrolling at these platforms and using these services. The early users should be paid and later joiners should be paid a little less. How much a user should be paid will also depend on how active the user is. In simple words, every user on a platform should be valued differently because the value that each of these users adds in making the platform successful is different and depends on their activity levels and the quality of their activities.

Should the users also get an "open offer"?

There are several countries where the takeover code, as prescribed by the market regulator, talks about an open offer. When a company acquires a significant stake in another listed entity, an open offer gets triggered. This means the acquiring company must make an offer to existing shareholders to buy their holdings at the same price that the acquirer is paying to the majority shareholders of the target company. It is aimed at giving the shareholders an exit option, as there may be a management change post-acquisition and investors may perceive potential risks in the business.

The other objective behind the open-offer rule is to ensure that, whenever majority shareholders are making higher returns (as a result of the acquisition price being higher than the market price before the acquisition was announced), minority shareholders should not be left behind and they too should get an opportunity to tender their shares if they think that the price that is being offered by the acquirer is fair.[9]

This may sound crazy but whenever larger companies acquire their smaller rivals in order to eliminate a possible future threat, users should also be paid by the acquirer. For example, when Facebook acquired WhatsApp, why did only a small group of employees and investors in WhatsApp benefit and not the users who made the app what it is?

The dark side of data

In an interesting article titled "There is a dark side to Big Data, and you can see it in the mirror"[10] in *Delaware Business Time*, Professor Dustin J. Sleesman highlights the other side of Big Data, which, in collecting and analyzing huge amounts of information is thereby affecting the speed and quality of humankind's decision-making choices. The supporters of this new technology claim that Big Data is the only answer for efficient, unbiased, quick and effective decision-making. But at the end of the day, this is only a tool that provides information: the use of that information to inform a decision is still dependant on how humans design the process.

This article mentions that, for example, due to strong confirmation bias, people are likely to use data merely to reinforce their own preconceived opinions. If you do not like the output of a statistical analysis, you may be tempted to tweak the parameters and recalculate the output. Humans also have a tendency to be over-confident in their abilities, which creates a problem when they are responsible for high-powered, complex Big Data tools. There are inherent cognitive biases that may sway people to misuse data analytics. These biases will either stop us from using Big Data techniques or they will make us trust them much less when we do not agree with the conclusions drawn by these systems.

There is also a practical problem. Another relevant issue discussed by the article is why professionals are sometimes reluctant to use decision-support tools like Big Data. These experts went through all that education, training and years of hard work to become skilled decision-makers in their respective fields. Are they really going to think it's fair or acceptable to relegate decisions to an algorithm or to computer software, especially when it disagrees with their personal assessments? There is also research suggests that customers or clients may even view a company negatively if it lets technology make decisions for it. Regardless of efficacy, many people don't feel comfortable letting technology steer their decisions.

This conclusion is not one-sided either. Some studies have even suggested that intuition can actually be more effective than rational analysis which is based on data and information for certain judgments, such as those involving creativity or morality. Intuition is also helpful when a quick decision is needed, especially when people have acquired domain expertise. Examples include firefighters making rapid assessments of how to extinguish a structural fire or neonatal nurses making snap judgments about the medical needs of a high-risk infant after birth. Intuition can easily score over Big Data in these cases.

Professor Sleesman writes about a study he conducted in which he and his colleagues studied US Air Force captains to examine the impact of leader intuition on team performance. The results indicated that in situations requiring a significant amount of information processing, teams achieved higher performance levels when leaders used intuition in decision-making, compared to those who did not. This may be the case because intuition helped these captains to develop a holistic, big-picture understanding of the complexities of their situation, enabling them to facilitate better team coordination and performance.

There are several areas where combining the strength of intuition with the insights of Big Data may be the best way forward. The article also leaves us with a warning that, despite all the hype, we shouldn't merely outsource decision-making to Big Data. We need to find ways of reducing the influence of cognitive biases that can lead data analytics astray, while at the same time leveraging the power of human intuition. Ultimately, the idea is to arrive at a better decision and not blindly follow a certain way of making it.

In the next chapter

In this chapter we looked at similarities between the creation of fixed assets followed by the expending of such assets using depreciation over a period of time and investment in Big Data with the objective of creating a competitive advantage which is followed by its use in generating more revenues and/or higher profitability. This requires that tech giants be taxed on the value of the data they own. Data is an asset which should be put on the balance sheet and any increase or decline captured in the income statement.

In the next chapter, we discuss the issues and questions around the ethics of Big Data. It would be dangerous to ignore the warning signs that suggest Big Data is leading to unfair advantages and unethical business practices, which include personalized pricing and costing products and services solely on the basis of a user's ability to pay, or on how desperately they need it. Profits can be maximized by the efficient use of Big Data but these practices are questionable, ethically, and there is little doubt that there needs to be a way to curtail them. Instead of empowering customers, Big Data may be empowering companies against their customers.

The other issue that we discuss in the next chapter is whether social media are influencing the working of democracy by distorting public opinion. Social media users are knowingly or unknowingly becoming less tolerant to different opinions or points of view that divergence from their own. As technology companies increasingly succeed by monetizing public attention, the consequences of an agenda-driven and artificially induced distortion of opinions are going to be grave for societies and their structures of governance.

Notes

1 Eli Pariser (born 17th December 1980) is the chief executive of Upworthy. He is an Internet activist, the board president of MoveOn.org and a co-founder of Avaaz.org. www.opensocietyfoundations.org/people/eli-pariser (accessed on 15th April 2019).
2 "Hack brief: Uber paid off hackers to hide a 57-million-user data breach" by Andy Greenberg.   www.wired.com/story/uber-paid-off-hackers-to-hide-a-57-million-user-data-breach (accessed on 6th December 2017).
   "Uber paid hackers to delete stolen data on 57 million people" by Eric Newcomer. www.bloomberg.com/news/articles/2017-11-21/uber-concealed-cyberattack-that-exposed-57-million-people-s-data (accessed on 6th December 2017).
   "Uber paid hackers $100,000 for silence on cyberattack that exposed 57 million people's data" by Biz Carson. www.forbes.com/sites/bizcarson/2017/11/21/uber-hack-payoff-57-million-data-exposed (accessed on 6th December 2017).
   "Uber: We paid hackers $100k to delete info on 57 million users last year" by Janet Burns. www.forbes.com/sites/janetwburns/2017/11/21/uber-we-paid-hackers-100k-to-delete-info-on-57-million-users-last-year/#63861a1b233f (accessed on 6th December 2017).
3 *Artificial Intelligence: Evolution, Ethics and Public Policy* by Saswat Sarangi and Pankaj Sharma (2019, Abingdon, Oxon: Routledge).
4 The Unique Identification Authority of India is a statutory authority established under the provisions of the Aadhaar Act 2016 by the Government of India under the Ministry of Electronics & Information Technology.
   https://uidai.gov.in/about-uidai/about-uidai.html (accessed on 4th December 2017).
5 "Depreciation" reviewed by Will Kenton. www.investopedia.com/terms/d/depreciation.asp (accessed on 30th September 2017).
6 "Enron scandal: The fall of a Wall Street darling" by Troy Segal. www.investopedia.com/updates/enron-scandal-summary (accessed on 15th April 2019).
   "Kenneth Lay: obituary." www.economist.com/node/7141201 (accessed on 9th December 2017).
7 "Regulating the internet giants." www.economist.com/news/leaders/21721656-data-economy-demands-new-approach-antitrust-rules-worlds-most-valuable-resource (accessed on 3rd October 2017).
8 "Network effect" reviewed by Caroline Banton www.investopedia.com/terms/n/network-effect.asp (accessed on 15th April 2019).
9 "What is an open offer?" by Masoom Gupte. www.business-standard.com/article/pf/what-is-an-open-offer-111051000079_1.html (accessed on 5th October 2017).
10 "Viewpoint: There is a dark side to Big Data, and you can see it in the mirror" by Dustin J. Sleesman. www.delawarebusinesstimes.com/viewpoint-dark-side-big-data-can-see-mirror (accessed on 24th February 2018).

9

BIG DATA

Is there a question mark over ethics?

> Data is not information, information is not knowledge, knowledge is not under-
> standing, understanding is not wisdom.
>
> — *Clifford Stoll*[1]

Are social media a threat to democracy?

There are several concerns about how social media is influencing the working of democracy and many publications have started to raise this issue repeatedly.[2] In one of its papers published in October 2017 the Omidyar Group wrote that it is becoming increasingly apparent that fundamental principles underlying democracy – trust, informed dialog, a shared sense of reality, mutual consent and participation – are being put to the test by certain features and attributes of social media. As technology companies increasingly achieve financial success by monetizing public attention, some of the key issues and unintended consequences arising as a result are important enough to be discussed in this context.

This paper also talked about six important issues: (1) social media has exacerbated polarization, (2) social media is instrumental in the spread of false and misleading information, (3) social media platforms convert popularity into legitimacy, (4) social media platforms allow and intensify manipulation by "populist" leaders, (5) the revenue model of social media channels is based on personal-data capture and targeted messaging or advertising and (6) some social media platforms have policies and features that enable unintended consequences which imply the encouragement of uncivil debate. All of this is combined with-less-than optimal democratic operations.

In its 4th November 2017 edition, *The Economist* in an article titled "Do social media threaten democracy?" wrote that Facebook, Google and Twitter were supposed to save politics due to good information driving out prejudice and falsehood.

However, something has gone very wrong with that premise. Social media held out the promise of a more enlightened politics, as accurate information and effortless communication helped good people drive out corruption, bigotry and lies. Yet Facebook acknowledged that before and after the 2016 US election, between January 2015 and August 2017, 146 million users may have seen Russian misinformation on its platform. Google's YouTube admitted to 1,108 Russian-linked videos and Twitter admitted to 36,746 similar accounts.

This means that there needs to be a check, with the help of a legal and regulatory framework, of social media companies so that the institutions which have evolved over several generations and still remain the best possible method of governance don't get damaged beyond repair. Living in denial may not help but accepting the challenge and making an effort to find the correct remedial measures is the only choice available to us.

Pricing manipulation at online retailers: it is legal but is it ethical?

The US retail industry is undergoing a crisis. Retail stores are closing on an almost daily basis and in large numbers. It is not that people have stopped buying things, but the shift to purchase online has proved to be the kiss of death for bricks-and-mortar stores. In a 4th December 2017 article titled "There are 170,000 fewer retail jobs in 2017 – and 75,000 more Amazon robots"[3] by Dave Edwards and Helen Edwards at *Quartz*, the authors talk in detail about the challenge of job losses. Their analysis suggests that the combined employment at Amazon and in Amazon-related retail would decline because of an increase in robots at Amazon. Amazon's growth and efficiency is getting better as the company is increasing its investment in robotics.

Amazon's share of the US e-commerce market is now 49%, or 5% of all retail spend. Amazon is set to clear $258.22 billion in US retail sales in 2018, according to eMarketer's figures, which will work out to 49.1 percent of all online retail spend in the country and 5% of all retail sales. Amazon's growing army of robots is highly effective at terminating human retail employees. However, there are subtle details to this issue that were not understood and appreciated in the past.

(1) Let us look at "specific to user" pricing. The price tags at online shopping sites aren't the same as bricks-and-mortar departmental stores. They change with a user's perceived ability to pay and so these are personalized prices. Online retailers have data about customers which has been collected over the years. On the basis of data collected on our online purchase habits, they can manipulate many things but most important among them is pricing. It is as simple as this: the price we will be asked to pay is a complex equation with numerous variables and the price we are going to pay will depend on our cumulative purchase behavior online.

(2) Apart from convenience, the most important reason why online retail picked up so quickly was *competitive pricing*. Buyers realized that they could get the best deals online and that pricing online is more competitive compared to

bricks-and-mortar stores. The assumption was that, since online stores can't attract buyers on the basis of their location, decor and available choices, they will offer customers better pricing.

As discussed in the recent article, "How online shopping makes suckers of us all" by Jerry Useem, published in *The Atlantic*[4] online retailers have already started using highly sophisticated ways to adjust and personalize prices to maximize profits. The article talks in great detail about how the price that extracts the most profit from a consumer has become a hot topic for a large number of researchers. These so-called "price experiments" have become a routine exercise because the right price can change by the day or even by the hour. Officially, though, not many companies would admit this. For example Amazon says its price changes are not attempts to gather data on customers' spending habits, but rather to give shoppers the lowest price out there.

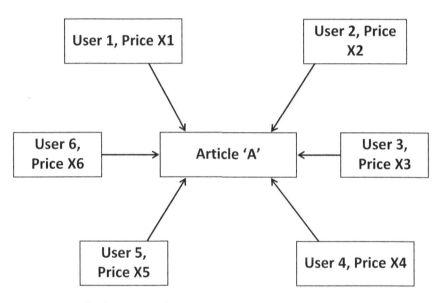

FIGURE 9.1   Individual Pricing for Every User

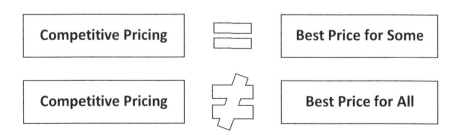

FIGURE 9.2   Price Discovery Online is Not the Most Optimal for Everyone

The article raises a fundamental question: could the Internet, whose transparency was supposed to empower consumers, be doing just the opposite?

When online merchants have the tools to dynamically adjust prices based on factors like where the customer is from and what the customer has been buying – at what price and how regularly – then online retailers have the power to create a demand–supply equation for an individual customer. Economics 101 has taught us the demand–supply equilibrium for the market as a whole but online retailers are taking it to an altogether higher level where the demand–supply equilibrium is not for the market but for the individual!

The implications are very interesting, or threatening, or frightening, depending on how you look at them. More granular data and consequent pricing decisions are good for online merchants and they can maximize profits and attain higher profits. But are they, collectively, also good and fair for customers? Look at it from another perspective: your neighborhood store always knew which brand of soft drink you liked but it never charged you a higher price for that on the basis of the information it had. But online retailers have the ability to do this and most people would not even realize it.

Not every person expresses the same demand for a product; different people have different levels of need for the same product. The enormous amount of data held by online retailers empowers them to dissect customer buying patterns and then effectively guide the individual's demand. There is no market equilibrium price in this new scenario; it is an equilibrium price for the individual.

There are many real-life instances of how pricing manipulation is possible according to the need and "desperation" of the customer. For example, how much will you pay for an air ticket when you have an emergency? What is the right price for a book you immediately need for your coursework?[5]

Scenario 1: how much will you pay for an air ticket?

Imagine you have an emergency in the family and you have to travel from Chicago to Boston and need to set out as early as you can. The airline companies may have access to your data (your phone calls, emails, Facebook posts) and may change pricing accordingly. The sophisticated and complex algorithms at the servers of these airlines can quote a fare to you on the basis of your urgent

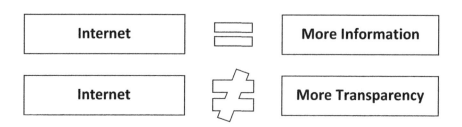

FIGURE 9.3   Information is Not Always Equal to Transparency

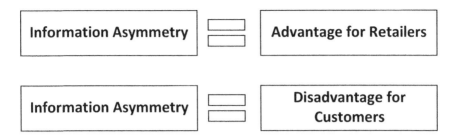

FIGURE 9.4   Information Asymmetry and Impact

need to travel. And this is not the same as expensive fares during holiday season because during holiday season, the market equilibrium itself shifts to a higher price because of higher demand. The result is: more revenues and higher profits for the airlines.

Scenario 2: what is the right price for a book you need?

Imagine you have just enrolled in college and you desperately need that *Advanced Mathematics* textbook because it is a part of prescribed reading for your course-work. You didn't have this need six months ago and you won't have this need six months from now. Hence, your willingness to pay a higher price for this book is at its maximum today compared to any other time. Online retailers can manipulate prices if they know, on the basis of your recent searches, that you are in desperate need of this book today. They are likely to quote a higher price to you and you would probably still buy the book. The result is: more revenues and higher profits for online retailers.

Free-market principles and the ethics of business – the larger question

As of now, there are no laws prohibiting online merchants from making such pric-ing changes. But, do we need pricing controls to stop such dynamic pricing on the basis of an individual's need and purchase history? We believe that most people may want the law to intervene to stop such pricing discrimination or exploitation of customer data for the merchant's gain.

The broader question is not just about the existing law, but about morals and ethics. Based on these parameters, the behavior of some online retailers would certainly fall into an ethically ambiguous zone. Today we are only scratching the surface in terms of what is possible with better algorithms and advanced Big Data tools. Imagine if Big Data becomes so powerful that by using it online merchants can quote a price which is different for everyone and also different at all points of time: what would our reaction be? The question we need, collectively, to ask is whether we can leave everything to free-market principles?

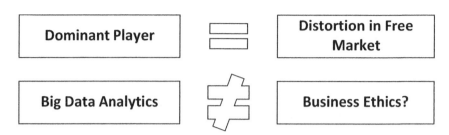

FIGURE 9.5 Dominant Player, Market Distortion and Business Ethics

Many companies, including Facebook, Google, Microsoft and Amazon are working on Big Data and its applications and it is an area which is not well understood by others, including customers, academics, governments and regulators. Not every company may be equally successful in the end but at least there is agreement on the fact that these companies have money to invest in Big Data. And of course, they have loads of money.

Big Data: the most potent force behind creating distortion in public opinion

The working algorithms of many of the public interaction and social media platforms are based on a sophisticated filtering mechanism. This filtering results in the fragmentation of users into clearly defined groups who don't interact with each other much. There is an inherent bias in these platforms to connect you only with people who think like you, agree with you and don't dissent much about sensitive and controversial issues.

For example, Facebook, as an advertising platform for its customers (the people buying advertising space on it) targets Facebook users to sell their products and services. However, selling products or services is one thing but distortion of public opinion can also be done with equal effectiveness. It is relatively easier as well. When you try selling a product or service to someone, the caution and defense mechanisms of the buyer are activated, which evaluate the product on its merits and may accept or reject it. The conversion or success rates of these attempts are very low.

However, it is a different story when you are reading or watching content on Facebook. When someone is browsing Facebook to read an article or watch a video with an agenda behind it and this user or viewer is not aware of it, the seller or advertiser of that content is likely to be far more successful in influencing the Facebook user's opinion. There is a difference between how cautious you are when you spend money (tangible) to buy a product compared to when you spend your time (intangible) to read or view something.

It is highly likely that the Facebook user may not even be aware and he or she is reading a piece which is targeted at him or her and is being paid for by someone else.

Even if it is not "paid-for content" and the piece is only being read by them because their user settings or recent likes led to Facebook algorithms figuring out which article or which video needs to be shown, the damage is already done. The user is floating in a loop where they only get to see what someone wants them see without even being aware of it most of the time.

Fake news: the genuine problem

It is hardly a surprise that, on many of these platforms, "fake news," which gets more clicks and thereby becomes more successful (because of gaining more popularity and also because it is virtually free to produce), drives out the *real* news, which often tells people things they are unwilling to hear and is much more expensive to produce. Another issue is that people have limited time and where they would only spend a limited number of minutes reading the news, Facebook is cannibalizing real newspaper and journals which are in the business of serious news. It is as simple as this: the more dependant people are on Facebook for their news and current affairs commentary, the worse it is for real and serious journalism in the world.

It is not entirely the fault of Facebook but an important point is that the effectiveness of Facebook is much higher than other media. It works better for advertisers because they can target their potential customers among Facebook users in a much smarter way. As well as customers, particular segments of voters can be targeted with complete precision. One instance from 2016 was an anti-Clinton ad repeating a notorious speech she made in 1996 on the subject of "super-predators." The advertisement was sent to African American voters in areas where the Republicans were trying, successfully as it turned out, to suppress the Democrat vote.[6]

There is also another serious issue linked to the deteriorating standards of public discourse. If the quality of public debate has lowered in recent years, a large part of the blame must go to online platforms where there are no authenticity checks and no verification of actual events. No one really seems to bother with the genuineness of news and people move on to the next item very quickly. It is good to talk about self-regulation but there is little evidence that it has been working. Should this be ignored by governments or should there be regulation for it? That is the question we have to think about.

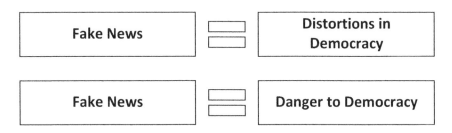

FIGURE 9.6   Fake News and its Impact on Democracy

Do tech companies just have too much data on users?

Companies like Facebook, Google, Amazon and Apple have so much information about their users that they have an almost complete profile of them. It may not be an exaggeration to say that Google and Facebook know their users more intimately than even their close friends or parents do. This leads to a situation where companies like Google and Facebook have a virtual monopoly on digital advertising. This has a snowballing effect. When a company has more users, it attracts more advertisers and makes more money. More money makes a company more powerful and it can invest more to attract even more users and in turn advertisers. It is fairly simple: from a company's perspective, it is a virtuous cycle. Any competitor starting afresh will find it very hard to compete.[7]

Big Data and competition

The application of competition law and policy to Big Data has become a major focus for government agencies around the world. Competition regulators around the world, from the US, to Japan, to the European Union have issued their own policy statements on the application of competition laws to Big Data. Big Data provides significant consumer benefits by encouraging companies to lower prices faster, encouraging innovative services to develop more quickly and allowing consumers to make more informed purchasing decisions.

For government authorities, it is important to address the concerns that the collection and use of consumer data by social media companies and online marketplaces can create market power which may not always be used for the benefit of customers. The collection and use of personal data raises novel issues for competition law. As the global economy becomes increasingly digitized, resolving these issues in a coherent and consistent manner will become even more important.[8]

Big Data and mass surveillance

There are concerns that the use of Big Data algorithms in the criminal justice system may lead to discriminatory practices. With more Big Data and AI, there will be more machine-driven decisions as governments use mass surveillance to gather data on people. On the basis of inputs from this surveillance, people are identified by their online activities and by data gathered from their activities in their offline "real life." There is a serious problem with this because racial profiling and other stereotypes could factor into mass surveillance.[9]

We are all partly responsible for this surveillance in the hyper-connected digital age, due to our constant updates, use of gadgets, apps, credit cards and everything in-between, making it easy for companies to track our every move glean insights into our personalities. But governments are not far behind; in fact they could be one step ahead because they are able to make such surveillance look like an initiative that is in the public interest. These seem to the guiding principles at the heart of China's new Social Credit System (SCS), for which implementation is underway. For creating an ideal society that is based on "trust" (quantifiably measured) and which promotes a culture of "sincerity," the SCS is a national reputation system that will, once fully functional, rate and rank every citizen.[10]

This ranking will be arrived at by tracking, monitoring, analyzing and evaluating every single thing a citizen does – who your friends are, where you buy from, what kinds of places you go to, have your bills been paid on time, everything – with each behavior rated either as positive or negative (desirable or undesirable, as defined by the government). All of this is then distilled into that citizen's rank, one single number that will determine the citizen's eligibility for everything from jobs to loans.

SCS: the proposed Chinese Government initiative

The SCS is an initiative, proposed by the Chinese Government, for developing a national reputation system for both individuals and businesses and, officially speaking, the objective is to bring more transparency to how people and businesses are seen. The system has been reported as being intended to assign a "social credit" rating to every citizen based on government data regarding their economic and social status. The SCS also works as a mass surveillance tool and uses Big Data analysis technology. At this point, the media focus is more on individuals but, in addition to individuals, the system is also meant to rate the businesses which are operating in the Chinese market.[11]

According to the overall "Planning outline for the construction of a SCS (2014–2020)" issued by the State Council, the SCS will focus on four areas: "honesty in government affairs," "commercial integrity," "societal integrity" and "judicial credibility." Essentially, all the desirable and undesirable traits and how an individual or a business performs against them, will be rated with the help of continuous and consistent data. The Chinese Government is not only serious about this initiative, it is also moving very fast on its development. It wants the basic structures of the SCS to be in place by 2020.

The Chinese Government has fast-tracked the implementation of the SCS System, resulting in the publication of numerous policy documents and plans since the main plan was issued in 2014, notwithstanding fears that if the SCS is implemented as envisioned it will constitute a new way of controlling both the behavior of individuals and of businesses. Ultimately, how the system will be used is not yet known but it is pointless to imagine that it could not be used as a tool for discrimination or as a threat to blackmail people.[12]

On the face of it, the Chinese SCS will be much more comprehensive than the UIDAI (or Aadhaar) initiative in India.[13] It is also real-time and, considering that Aadhaar has led to a huge debate on privacy concerns, the implications of the Chinese SCS are not difficult to imagine.[14] It is impossible to escape from this surveillance unless you are ready to withdraw from "civilization." And with that there could be more trouble coming your way as it is likely that your act of hiding will count as a suspicious activity and you would be identified as a potential threat, as someone who needs to be watched even more closely.

The fact is that that this is how we might have to live in the future. But does it really look very different from the time US President George W. Bush[15] said, after the 9/11 attacks on the USA,[16] "Either you are with us, or you are with the terrorists."[17] Similarly, there is no room for neutrality here and, unfortunately, there is no middle path. The people who express concerns over privacy and the violation of human rights are immediately accused of supporting anti-social activities and criminals by more aggressive elements from the surveillance set-up or its supporters. This is worrying but with governments and companies amassing so much power, it is unlikely to change for the better.

In the next chapter

In this chapter, we looked at some of the ethical questions which are relevant for Big Data. As these technologies get more powerful, the risk of misuse increases. The immense commercial interests driven by human greed, combined with information asymmetry, make a lethal combination. This might be true for everyone and everything but what makes the major difference, metaphorically, is whether people are fighting with stones and axes, bullets and missiles, or nuclear weapons. The level of safeguards needed should vary according to this.

In the next chapter, we look at how Big Data may evolve in the future. There are already signs that it has become more powerful than it should have or should be, but the bad news is that it will continue to become more potent and the threat to privacy will become more real. Any solace can be found in the fact that the applications running on Big Data will become more convenient, including not just existing products and services but also newer ones that will become available. No one can really guarantee how successful the checks and balances will be or how sophisticated they will become but the backlash that tech companies will face is going to increase significantly. Regulators will not remain silent and they will continue to act in a manner that will seem harsh to many.

Notes

1 Clifford Paul "Cliff" Stoll is an American astronomer and author. He is known for his 1986 investigation, while working as a systems administrator at the Lawrence Berkeley National Laboratory, which led to the capture of the hacker Markus Hess and for his book *The Cuckoo's Egg*, in which he details the investigation. www.keynotes.org/speaker/CliffordStoll (accessed on 15th April 2019).
2 "Is social media a threat to democracy?" by Anamitra Deb (Director, Omidyar Network), Stacy Donohue (Investment Partner, Omidyar Network) and Tom Glaisyer (Program Director, Democracy Fund). In this paper, The Omidyar Group examined key issues and implications presented by social media participation and manipulation. www.omidyargroup.com/wp-content/uploads/2017/10/Social-Media-and-Democracy-October-5-2017.pdf (accessed on 6th December 2017).

"Scandal, outrage and politics: Do social media threaten democracy?" Leader piece. www.economist.com/news/leaders/21730871-facebook-google-and-twitter-were-supposed-save-politics-good-information-drove-out (accessed on 6th December 2017).

"6 ways social media has become a direct threat to democracy" by Pierre Omidyar. www.washingtonpost.com/news/theworldpost/wp/2017/10/09/pierre-omidyar-6-ways-social-media-has-become-a-direct-threat-to-democracy (accessed on 6th December 2017).

"Is social media a threat to democracy?" by Tom Glaisyer. www.democracyfund.org/blog/entry/is-social-media-a-threat-to-democracy (accessed on 6th December 2017).

3 "There are 170,000 fewer retail jobs in 2017 – and 75,000 more Amazon robots" by Dave Edwards and Helen Edwards. https://qz.com/1107112/there-are-170000-fewer-retail-jobs-in-2017-and-75000-more-amazon-robots/?mc_cid=2b276d770e&mc_eid=03ec13b62a (accessed on 7th December 2017).

4 "How online shopping makes suckers of us all" by Jerry Useem. *The Atlantic*, May 2017. www.theatlantic.com/magazine/archive/2017/05/how-online-shopping-makes-suckers-of-us-all/521448 (accessed on 22nd November 2017).

5 *Artificial Intelligence: Evolution, Ethics and Public Policy* by Saswat Sarangi and Pankaj Sharma (2019, Abingdon, Oxon: Routledge).

6 "Why Hillary's super-predator comment matters" by Ronda Lee. www.huffingtonpost.com/ronda-lee/hillarys-superpredator-comment_b_9655052.html (accessed on 9th December).

"Did Hillary Clinton call African American youth 'superpredators?'" by Allison Graves. www.politifact.com/truth-o-meter/statements/2016/aug/28/reince-priebus/did-hillary-clinton-call-african-american-youth-su (accessed on 9th December).

"1996: Hillary Clinton on 'superpredators'" (C-SPAN). Complete clip of Hillary Clinton's 1996 reference to "superpredators." www.youtube.com/watch?v=j0uCrA7ePno (accessed on 9th December).

"Hillary Clinton the racist." Forum topic. http://theramshuddle.com/topic/hillary-clinton-the-racist/ (accessed on 9th December).

7 "You are the product" book review by John Lanchester. *The London Review of Books*. Covering: *The Attention Merchants: From the Daily Newspaper to Social Media, How Our Time and Attention Is Harvested and Sold* by Tim Wu; *Chaos Monkeys: Inside the Silicon Valley Money Machine* by Antonio García Martínez; *Move Fast and Break Things: How Facebook, Google and Amazon have Cornered Culture and What It Means for All of Us* by Jonathan Taplin. www.lrb.co.uk/v39/n16/john-lanchester/you-are-the-product (accessed on 30th October 2017).

8 "Canadian competition policy focuses in on "Big Data." by Blake Cassels & Graydon LLP. www.lexology.com/library/detail.aspx?g=140bcc47-fd72-44f2-ba18-e6ac7647785f (accessed on 24th February 2018).

9 "The introduction of new technology brings changes to U.S. criminal justice system" by Abby Doeden. https://badgerherald.com/news/2018/02/23/visiting-professors-express-concerns-on-how-big-data-mass-surveillance-will-affect-criminal-justice-system (accessed on 24th February 2018).

10 "When Big Brother meets Big Data, we get to live in glass houses!" by Gautham Shenoy. https://factordaily.com/big-brother-big-data (accessed on 25th February 2018).

11 "China has started ranking citizens with a social credit system" by Alexandra Ma. www.businessinsider.in/China-has-started-ranking-citizens-with-a-creepy-social-credit-system-heres-what-you-can-do-wrong-and-the-embarrassing-demeaning-ways-they-can-punish-you/articleshow/63666457.cms (accessed on 15th April 2019).

12 "China rates its own citizens – including online behavior" by Fokke Obbema, Marije Vlaskamp and Michael Persson. www.volkskrant.nl/buitenland/china-rates-its-own-citizens-including-online-behaviour~a3979668 (accessed on 25th February 2018).

13 "Big Data meets Big Brother as China moves to rate its citizens" by Rachel Botsman. www.wired.co.uk/article/chinese-government-social-credit-score-privacy-invasion (accessed on 25th February 2018).

"China's new tool for social control: A credit rating for everything" by Josh Chin and Gillian Wong. www.wsj.com/articles/chinas-new-tool-for-social-control-a-credit-rating-for-everything-1480351590 (accessed on 25th February 2018).

14 "China 'social credit:' Beijing sets up huge system" by Celia Hatton. www.bbc.com/news/world-asia-china-34592186 (accessed on 25th February 2018); "Behind the fire-wall: How China tamed the internet" by Simon Denyer. www.washingtonpost.com/world/asia_pacific/chinas-plan-to-organize-its-whole-society-around-big-data-a-rating-for-everyone/2016/10/20/1cd0dd9c-9516-11e6-ae9d-0030ac1899cd_story.html?utm_term=.b158c2abf4b7 (accessed on 25th February 2018).

15 George Walker Bush is an American politician who served as the 43rd President of the United States from 2001 to 2009. He was also the 46th Governor of Texas from 1995 to 2000. Bush is a member of a prominent political family and is the eldest son of Barbara and George H.W. Bush, the 41st President of the United States. www.biography.com/people/george-w-bush-9232768 (accessed on 15th April 2019).

16 The "September 11 attacks" (also referred to as "9/11") were a series of four coordinated terrorist attacks by the Islamic terrorist group al-Qaeda on the United States on the morning of 11th September 2001. The attacks killed 2,996 people, injured over 6,000 and caused at least $10 billion worth of infrastructure and property damage. www.history.com/topics/21st-century/9-11-timeline (accessed on 25th February 2018).

17 "Bush: 'You are either with us, or with the terrorists'" (no author). Voice of America. www.voanews.com/a/a-13-a-2001-09-21-14-bush-66411197/549664.html (accessed on 25th February 2018).

10

THE FUTURE OF BIG DATA

> There was 5 Exabytes of information created between the dawn of civilization through 2003, but that much information is now created every 2 days, and the pace is increasing.
>
> *— Eric Schmidt*[1]

A treadmill running faster and faster

There are more than seven billion of us who belong to humankind and while we may not all be using a smartphone or have an Internet connection, the number of people who do not is consistently and continuously declining. Most people, from morning till night, continue to generate and consume data. Beginning from booking a cab through ride-hailing applications, checking social media accounts, ordering food online, consuming media content on websites and apps, booking the evening play or a movie, ordering groceries, making bookings for dinner and uploading pictures onto social media before going to sleep, the data is ubiquitous.

More is available, more is consumed and the treadmill continues to pick up speed. And just imagine: humans alone are the not the consumers of data, it is the machines surrounding us that are storing and analyzing a gigantic stream of data. For example, the hundreds of thousands of CCTV cameras used in video surveillance across shopping malls, housing complexes, airports, train stations, offices, individual houses and other public places continue to record huge amounts of data. Social media platforms continue to remain active 24/7 and in the process keep generating, storing and analyzing large amounts of data.

History has enough evidence to show that large-scale technological changes have an irreversible impact on the world and its inhabitants. They change our habits, they change the way we live and, in the process, they change everything associated with ourselves. If we could travel backwards in time to see how people used to live 500 years ago, it would be almost unrecognizable to us. Since the pace of change is getting faster, if we were somehow able to sneak a glance at the life of humans hundreds of years from now, it would also look completely different to us. This is the story with data as well. Data became Big Data and it is getting bigger and bigger. The most important issue is how this change will occur and, while there is nothing more ridiculous than forecasting in complex situations like these, we still think there would be some broad identifiable trends.

Big Data and analytics will get stronger

That Big Data will continue to get more powerful is hardly in question. The speed at which it will be generated, be processed and be analyzed to produce meaningful inferences will increase. It is obvious that Big Data will continue to become more powerful and the speed at which it will be generated, processed and analyzed to produce meaningful inferences will only increase. Since data is at the core of most of the things you hear or talk about in the realm of new technology, it will continue to grow more valuable and important. This is true for blockchain, machine learning, the Internet of Things (IoT), AI or products like smart watches and smart televisions. The result is that Big Data will continue to get stronger and our dependency on it will also continue to increase. Another downside could be that new and changed mindsets, approaches and skills may become redundant as quickly as they become valuable. The pace of change will be very high and as an individual, or as an organization, or for a government, there will be an ongoing need to be dynamic and open to change. People will need to be agile in their thinking. The pecking order for relevant and specific methods and technologies will continue to change and evolve and all of us will have to be sensitive to this.

Big Data applications will get better

Look at almost everything around you that runs on data. In most cases, these applications are getting better despite continuously swelling numbers of users. Services are getting faster and more personalized. In this context, Google Maps, for example, is an interesting example in terms of coverage, areas mapped, the level of detailing and the algorithms on which its forecasts are based. Another dimension to this is how more and more organizations are becoming sensitive to the importance of data and the kind of impact it can make. Investments are increasing, more and better talent is being hired and, as a result, there are more and more options available for end users and customers to choose from. This will only grow faster and stronger. There will be more applications and services benefiting from Big Data available to ordinary people as they shift from research labs to become commercial applications. This will be a major driving force for the direction the global economy will take.

Privacy will be an even bigger casualty

As things stand today, the threat to an individual's privacy is one of the major downsides of this technology. While there are attempts to address this, they will remain unorganized, as the power balance lies with the people who gain from this negative consequence: major companies that benefit directly and the businesses that make profit while your data remains with them. Governments benefit from knowing more about you and there will always be people and sections of the media who believe that "the security of the majority is more important than the privacy of the minority." The most interesting aspect is that different entities (technology companies, other businesses, governments, cybercriminals) will have different reasons for why they need to have access to data, but the end result will be the same: you and your data will remain vulnerable. There is unlikely to be a major respite on this, no matter how much it is emphasized.

There will be a regulatory backlash

Globally, there is already a backlash against how Big Data and its beneficiaries (in the form of tech companies) are using it and how it is impacting society. There are also serious concerns about how much respect many of these beneficiaries have for the individual's privacy. Questions are also being asked about how these virtual monopolies are affecting the competitive landscape in their areas of business and how this influences the choices available to users and customers. Regulators also worry about how much these companies abuse their positions and how best to address these challenges. All of these are complex issues and there are no straightforward answers. However, it is unlikely that the main users of Big Data will avoid being at the receiving end of regulations and, in most situations, you can't blame anyone else but them. The general perception is that many of these companies first try to hide any breaches or wrongdoings; they deny any guilt if negative information becomes public and, if they have to accept that they are indeed guilty, they try to find ways to get off lightly. Globally, governments, regulators and law enforcement agencies will continue to target them and the regulatory backlash will get more intense, frequent and powerful.

The "psychological impact" will come under more scrutiny

The debate on the psychological impact of Big Data has already begun. There have been discussions on how social media, e-commerce and many other Big Data applications are impacting communities and how they are influencing the individual. There are several warning signs already and there are many agencies and independent experts expressing concern about the possible impact being seen in the behavioral patterns of people. There are questions about the possible impact of how much time they spend online, how they interact with others in the virtual world and how aggressive they can be. The rising levels of intolerance to different viewpoints, due to the way in which many of these platforms work like "echo chambers," could have serious implications not just for the safety and security of people with unpopular opinions but such attitudes may also harm the basic tenets of equality. It is very likely that such issues around Big Data will be debated more and more in future as people will become more sensitized to the possible consequences.

Finally, how scientific history will judge Big Data depends on what we do today

Humankind has progressed because men and women have the habit of continuously challenging the status quo, looking beyond the obvious and debating everything. *Homo sapiens* are always thinking and making critical reassessments and this has been the foundation of scientific progress and a world that is more peaceful, more prosperous and more healthy than at any point in history. People tend not to fear the unfamiliar and scientists and researchers are not afraid of venturing into unchartered territories. This philosophy has worked extremely well in the past.

Big Data as a technology is the result of immense scientific progress, particularly in computing and mathematics and it is opening up new vistas. The opportunities and benefits are much greater than the threats and drawbacks. As computers continue to get faster and faster, data storage capacities continue to increase and algorithms become more advanced, Big Data and analytics have the potential to make fundamental positive differences in human life and, along with progress in other related and dependant technologies, this will be one of the great influencers in the future. The only thing we need to be careful about is to keep looking out for potential catastrophes, because one such terrible event could be far more powerful than thousands of Big Data blessings.

Notes

1 "The web is much bigger (and smaller) than you think" by Bruce Upbin. A guest post by Gary Griffiths, CEO and co-founder of Trapit, a personalized content discovery platform. Trapit was incubated at SRI and the CALO project. www.forbes. com/sites/ciocentral/2012/04/24/the-web-is-much-bigger-and-smaller-than-you-think/#2cb539876194 (accessed on 17th April 2019).

   Eric (Emerson) Schmidt (born 27th April 1955, Washington, D.C.) is an American information technology executive who served as chairman and CEO of Google Inc. In March 2001, Schmidt was hired by Google as board chairman. Less than five months later he was given the additional title of CEO. At this time, Google's two founders, Larry Page and Sergey Brin, became president of products and president of technology, respectively. Schmidt oversaw Google's initial public offering in August 2004 and also served as a company spokesperson. www.britannica.com/biography/Eric-Schmidt (accessed on 18th April 2019).

EPILOGUE

You can have data without information, but you cannot have information without data.

— Daniel Keys Moran[1]

Big Data has arrived

NewVantage Partners[2] carries out a survey every year called the "Annual Big Data Executive Survey"[3] and it talks to senior executives about the links between data and innovation and how Big Data and artificial intelligence (AI) are driving business innovation. The 2018 survey confirms that AI and Big Data are now a well-established focus at most of these large and sophisticated firms. There is a stronger feeling that Big Data and AI projects deliver value and a greater concern that established firms will be disrupted by start-ups much more in the future than was observed in past surveys.[4]

No matter what we call it, there is a serious data explosion and an urgent need to make sense of it. The latest survey identifies that Big Data and AI projects have become virtually indistinguishable, particularly given that machine learning is one of the most popular techniques for dealing with large volumes of fast-moving data. It's also the case that statistical approaches to AI – deep learning, for example – are increasingly popular. Therefore, traditional data analytics, Big Data and AI are part of a continuum.

Virtually all of the respondents (97%) say they are investing in these types of projects. Companies continue to derive value from their Big Data and AI projects, with 73% of respondents saying they have already received measurable value from these initiatives. This number is higher than in the 2017 survey, which suggests that more value is being achieved as companies grow familiar with the technologies involved. The types of value received are perhaps consistent with other previous types of technology. Big Data and AI are extensions of analytical capabilities, the most common objectives – and those most likely to achieve success – are "advanced analytics/better decisions." Better customer service and reducing costs are also common objectives.

The 2018 survey also confirms that innovation happens at the edges: where a few firms lead, many others will follow. A subset of firms (over a quarter, or 27%), are prioritizing innovation initiatives – innovation/disruption, speed-to-market and monetization – but innovation remains an aspiration for most large enterprises. Over half of respondents (53.6%) confirm that they are undertaking innovation initiatives in at least one of these areas. However, data monetization, which has been a stated objective of many firms, remains a relatively low priority (7.2%) with a low success rate (8.7%) at this time.

One of the greatest areas of concern in the survey, for large enterprises, is the risk of disruption from new entrants. Almost four out of five respondents said they feared disruption or displacement from firms like those in the "fintech" sector or from firms specializing in Big Data. The technology judged most disruptive is, by far, AI. Seventy-two percent chose it as the disruptive technology with the most impact – far more than cloud computing (13%) or blockchain (7%). Another important and continuing issue is the slow speed with which these established firms make the shift to a data-driven culture. Virtually all respondents say their firms are trying to make the shift, but only about one-third have already managed this. This issue is emphasized every year and doesn't improve much.

Clearly, firms need more concerted programs to achieve data-related cultural change. Many start-ups have established data-driven cultures from the beginning, which is a key reason why more established firms fear disruption from them. One of the approaches that firms have taken to try to deal with data-driven disruption and change is to establish new management roles. Every year, for example, the percentage of firms with Chief Data Officers (CDO) rises. However, there is still a lack of clarity about how different data-oriented roles relate to each other and even what types of backgrounds are appropriate for CDO jobs.

Role-clarity is critical for both leading AI/Big Data projects and for accomplishing cultural change. And while all respondents believed it was important, the majority of firms still lack an enterprise data strategy. This continuing rise in the importance and challenges of Big Data is one of the most important features of contemporary economy and society. The survey emphasizes that the key to success is to determine how firms should respond and then to move ahead to execute the necessary changes in a systematic and effective fashion.

If there were any doubts about the relevance of Big Data for the corporate world today, this survey makes it clear that data analytics, Big Data and AI are widely seen by banks, manufacturers and technology firms as part of a big technological transformation as they begin to derive value while at the same time encountering increased competition from data-driven start-ups. Machine learning and other automated approaches are deployed to cope with large volumes of fast-moving data. However, the future path is unlikely to be smooth as several organizations continue to struggle with changes in their culture and challenges related to problems with the management of human resources.[5]

Developing countries are also catching up quickly with the new technology. For example, according to an Oracle survey,[6] Big Data space, adoption, customer interaction and operational excellence are growing rapidly among Indian enterprises as Indian companies are adopting new technologies to improve operations and enhance customer experience at a greater pace than the rest of the Asia-Pacific (APAC) countries. According to a survey conducted by the market research firm Longitude Research[7] along with Oracle and chip maker Intel,[8] the cloud strategies of 43% of Indian businesses are fully implemented and working.[9]

The survey added that an emerging group of businesses that have 70% or more of their applications in the cloud are out-performing their competitors globally. Businesses in India are now looking to capitalize on new and innovative technologies, such as open-source, multi-platform capabilities and visual tools in the next year. Nearly a quarter (23%) of IT executives from India felt that automation capabilities were important to their business and one-fifth underlined the importance of AI and machine learning (ML) within their organizations. According to Oracle, ML, AI and Big Data analytics will become intrinsic to every point in an organization in order to make it future-ready.

The message is loud and clear: there is no escape from this technology and its far-reaching implications. Big Data is here and will make an indelible, permanent impact in the coming decades on several aspects of our lives, including business, politics, society, the economy and almost everything else. You will have to adapt or perish. This doesn't just apply to organizations, this applies to governments, individuals, societies, countries and economies . . . for humankind at large.

Notes

1 Daniel Keys Moran is an American computer programmer and a popular science fiction writer. https://danielkeysmoran.blogspot.com (accessed on 27th April 2019); www.amazon.com/Daniel-Keys-Moran/e/B000APWTIG (accessed on 27th April 2019).

2 NewVantage Partners are advisors in Big Data and business innovation. Since 2001, NewVantage Partners have worked with companies in leveraging data and analytics to drive innovation and business results. NewVantage Partners are based in Boston with offices in New York, San Francisco, Austin and Charlotte. http://newvantage.com (accessed on 25th February 2018).

3 In January 2018, NewVantage Partners released the results of its 6th Annual Big Data Executive Survey, titled "Data and innovation: How Big Data and AI are driving business innovation." The Survey reports on the evolution of executive perspectives from nearly 60 Fortune 1,000 companies, as firms come to terms with the impact of Big Data and its implications. www.businesswire.com/news/home/20180108005172/en/NewVantage-Partners-Releases-Annual-Big-Data-Executive (accessed on 25th February 2018).

4 "Big Data executive survey 2018: Executive summary of findings" from the foreword by Thomas H. Davenport and Randy Bean. http://newvantage.com/wp-content/uploads/2018/01/Big-Data-Executive-Survey-2018-Findings.pdf (accessed on 25th February 2018).

5 "AI, Big Data are meshing – And disrupting" by George Leopold (20th Feb 2018) on Datanami. www.datanami.com/2018/02/20/ai-big-data-meshing-disrupting (accessed on 25th February 2018).

6 The Oracle Corporation is a multinational computer technology corporation, headquartered in California. The company specializes in developing and marketing database software and technology, cloud engineered systems and enterprise software products.

The company also develops and builds tools for database development and systems of middle-tier software, enterprise resource planning (ERP) software, customer relationship management (CRM) software and supply-chain management (SCM) software. www.oracle.com/index.html (accessed on 27th April 2019).

7 Longitude is a research firm headquartered in London, UK. It specializes in advisory and research services for corporate clients. Longitude's core services relate to the production of white papers, research reports and supporting content across many sectors including IT; energy; banking and finance; telecommunications; healthcare; legal; retail and consumer goods; and manufacturing. www.longitude.co.uk (accessed on 27th April 2019).

8 Intel is a technology company headquartered in Santa Clara, California, in Silicon Valley. It invented the x86 series of microprocessors, which are the processors found in most PCs. Intel supplies processors for computer-system manufacturers such as Apple, Lenovo, HP and Dell. Intel also manufactures motherboard chipsets, network interface controllers, integrated circuits, flash memory, graphics chips, embedded processors and other devices related to communications and computing. Intel was founded on 18th July 1968, by Robert Noyce and Gordon Moore. www.intel.com/content/www/us/en/homepage.html (accessed on 27th April 2019).

9 "India tops Big Data and analytics adoption in APAC region: Oracle." The article states that the next-generation trends in the Big Data space, adoption, customer interaction and operational excellence are growing rapidly at Indian enterprises. www.thenewsminute.com/article/india-tops-big-data-and-analytics-adoption-apac-region-oracle-76972 (accessed on 25th February 2018).

INDEX

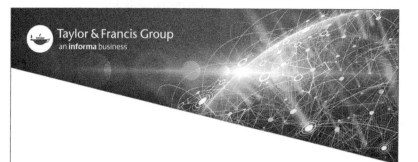

Made in the USA
Middletown, DE
02 October 2024

61929158R00080